"Catholic literature, doctrinal and devotional, owes a great deal to Mother Mary Loyola. There is a certain wholesomeness, naturalness, geniality about her spirituality that at once wins a place in the Catholic heart for whatever she writes." --The Ecclesiastical Review, volume 58, January 1918

About Mother Mary Loyola:

Most Catholics today who have heard the name Mother Mary Loyola know her as the author of *The King of the Golden City*, which has enjoyed a resurgence in popularity in recent years. But few know that she wrote over two dozen works, and that she was once a household name among Catholics of her era. What made her unique among Catholic authors was her ability to draw in her listeners with story after story—and not just any stories, but ones that incorporated current events and brand new inventions of the time. Despite the fact that those events are no longer current, and those inventions no longer brand new, her books scintillate with the appeal of an active mind that could find a moral in the most unusual places. And while the printed word lacks the animated facial expressions and vocal inflections which reveal a gifted storyteller, hers convey her enthusiasm so capably that the reader can easily imagine sitting at the feet of this wise old nun.

About *Trust*:

Mother Loyola remained vigorous into her later years, until in 1923, at the age of 78, she suffered a fall that resulted in a serious hip fracture. Without the benefit of hip surgery to relieve the pain, she was confined to her bed for the remaining years of her life. Undaunted, she continued to receive visitors and to write prolifically, penning *With the Church*, a two-volume set of meditations for the liturgical year, as well as numerous pamphlets for the Catholic Truth Society. Her final work, *Trust*, published in 1928, amply illustrates her state of mind as she approached her end: a keen awareness of the need for a childlike trust in God's Will for us, whatever that Will may be.

To learn more about Mother Mary Loyola, visit our website at
www.staugustineacademypress.com.

Learning to Embrace our Cross

Trust

BY

Mother Mary Loyola

WITH A PREFACE BY
Rev. Herbert F. Thurston, S.J.

2014
ST. AUGUSTINE ACADEMY PRESS
Homer Glen, Illinois

This book is newly typeset based on the edition published in 1928 by Benziger Brothers. All editing strictly limited to the correction of errors in the original text and minor clarifications in punctuation or phrasing. Any remaining oddities of spelling or phrasing are as found in the original.

Nihil Obstat
THOMAS MCLAUGHLIN, S.T.D.
Censor Deputatus

Imprimatur
EDM. CAN.SURMONT
Vic. Gen.

Westmonasterii, die 5° Novembris 1928.

This book was originally published in 1928 by Benziger Brothers. This edition ©2014 by St. Augustine Academy Press. All editing by Lisa Bergman.

ISBN: 978-1-936639-30-4
Library of Congress Control Number: 2014951768

Unless otherwise noted, all illustrations in this book, including the cover, are either the original illustrations as found in the book, or are public domain images.

To the Children Martyrs of All Time

AND

To the Little Ones of Our Own Day

IN WHOM

Love and Trust

Blossom

into Sanctity

Contents

Preface by Father Thurston, S.J.	ix
Foreword	xi
Trust in God—Creator	1
Trust in God—Repairer	7
Trust in God—Redeemer	13
Trust in His Omnipotence	21
Trust in His Fatherhood	32
Trust in His Wisdom	42
Trust in His Will	50
Trust in His Mercy	56
Trust in His Love	67
Trust in His Tests (I) "tutors and Governors"	75
Trust in His Tests (II) His Invitations	81
Trust in His Tests (III) His Promises to Prayer	90
Trust in His Tests (IV) His Discipline of Suffering	112
Trust in His Perpetual Mediation	131
Trust in His Reward—Himself	139

Preface

FAITH and Hope go hand in hand, and, with the decay of Faith, the Christian spirit of trust in God's Goodness, and in God's Providence, which was never more needed than at the present time, seems to be well nigh extinguished in the hearts of the rival majority. Almost a century has elapsed since the poet wrote:

> I falter where I firmly trod,
>   And falling with my weight of cares
>   Upon the great world's altar-stairs
> That slope through darkness up to God,
>
> I stretch lame hands of faith, and grope,
>   And gather dust, and chaff, and call
>   To what I feel is Lord of all,
> And faintly trust the larger hope.

    To those in like case the simple, prayerful teaching of the pages which follow will surely bring relief. These are not the unverified speculations of one who would strike out new paths, but they are the lessons of an experience as old as Christianity. They have been learnt in the school which our Lord Himself has indicated. Has He not said: "Amen I say to you, unless you be converted and become as little children you shall not enter into the kingdom of heaven"? And again, "whoever shall humble himself as this little child, he is the greater in the kingdom of heaven"? During the many years in which Mother Mary Loyola by voice and pen has laboured for God's little ones, we cannot be wrong in thinking that she has not only taught, but that she herself has learnt. We have to go to school to our children, but we understand their language with difficulty and we need an interpreter. Most of all we require someone to expound to us that which is most beautiful and most unique in childhood—its trustfulness. We are not likely, I am convinced, to find an intermediary who is better qualified for such a task than the author of the pages before us.

Herbert Thurston, S.J.

Foreword

AMONG beautiful creations in the spiritual order, few are more captivating than the miracles of grace in the souls of the very young. Perhaps it is the contrast they offer to the signs of the times, their rebuke to a self-sufficient and sophisticated age, that we find so refreshing. Anyway, we welcome them with wonder and delight. "There will be children saints," said Pope Pius XI, noting this as a characteristic feature of days when in greater measure than ever the Divine Householder is bringing out of His treasury new things and old.

The spiritual life of these little ones must be simplicity itself. It is but the blossoming out of their Baptism, the result of their happy privilege as children of God. He has given them all that they have and are, and they acknowledge His gifts by love and trust, the only way open to children, but covering all worship. Hand in hand with their heavenly Father, they pass swiftly through this world, undazzled by its allurements, untarnished by its touch, in a joyous familiarity with Him, which aged saints might envy and angels must admire.

> Life sees them spotless in Thy sight—and Death—
> What is it but the lifting them to Thee,
> Still in the fragrance of their purity!

Supernaturalized and expanded by Baptism, love and trust, the unspoilt instincts of the child suffice to make these children saints.

During His life on earth, our Lord delighted in the company of little children. Because of their innocence and simplicity and because of the opportunity they gave Him of showing His tenderness towards us, He loved to have them about Him. He blessed and caressed them and proposed them as teachers and models even to Apostles. He gave thanks to His Eternal Father for revealing to little ones things that are hidden from the "wise and prudent." We must not, then, disdain to learn from their guileless lips when they teach us their own characteristic lesson of trust.

"I know," said one of these little ones, "that God can do everything He wants, if I ask Him to. If I could pray well enough, I could change the moon into the sun."

We smile, yet envy the simplicity that overleaps the goal to which our wisdom and prudence will never attain.

We are all of us God's children and shall find some day that, in spite of the trials He has sent or permitted, we have been treated "as most dear children," and tenderly dealt with every one. Shall we study some of His tender ways that we may give Him the return a father asks and expects—love, loyalty, and unquestioning trust?

· T R U S T ·

I

Trust in God—Creator

> "Why hath God commanded you that you should not eat of every tree of paradise?"—Gen. 3:1

A SPANISH child, hearing for the first time of Eve's conversation with the serpent, exclaimed: "She oughtn't to have spoken to him. She should have made the Sign of the Cross and gone down another walk!"

There is a slight anachronism certainly; but the outburst of indignant zeal is admirable. That "Why?" of the tempter was a challenge. It should have roused to vigilance all that was needed for protection—horror at the audacity, loyalty, trust in God, silent scorn, prudence, and the instantaneous flight of occasion. Spain is famous for her theologians!

We can hardly help contrasting intuitions such us these—first-fruits of the unspoilt heart—with the ignoble instincts finding voice in England today. Our Lord's words come to mind: "I confess to thee, O Father, Lord of heaven and earth, because thou hast hid these things from the wise and prudent and hast revealed them to little ones. Yea, Father, for so hath it seemed good in thy sight!"

That "Why?" follows immediately upon the warning: "Now the serpent was more subtle than any of the beasts of the earth which the Lord God had made." By his very subtlety he has overreached himself many a time. The question here was detestable in its motive, but valuable for the answers it suggests:

Why should the Creator command the work of His hands?

The insolence horrified even a child. But one answer may be vouchsafed. God gives us His commands out of love. Having given us being, He would bring us safely to eternal life by guarding us amid the perils of the way, especially against the fatal self-seeking which since the Fall, constitutes our chief danger. "We see only a little way; God sees all the way home." Hidden snares, tempting but dangerous paths, our intemperate desires, our cowardly fears—all these He sees, and as the most solicitous of fathers He warns and commands.

There are some touching passages in Scripture which show the loving provision of God for His second creation, that after the fall of the rebel angels was to succeed to the heavenly places these had forfeited.

"In the beginning God created heaven and earth.... And He said: Let us make man to our own image and likeness.... And God created man to His own image: to the image of God He created him: male and female He created them. And God blessed them, saying: Increase and multiply, and fill the earth, and subdue it...and rule over all living creatures that move upon the earth.[1]

---

1 Gen. 1:1

"And the Lord God had planted a paradise of pleasure. And He brought forth of the ground all manner of trees, fair to behold and pleasant to eat of, and the tree of knowledge of good and evil. And the Lord God put man into the paradise of pleasure to dress it and to keep it.... And He commanded him saying: Of every tree of paradise thou shalt eat: but of the tree of the knowledge of good and evil thou shalt not eat. For in what day thou shalt eat of it thou shalt die the death."[1]

"He gave them counsel and a heart to devise…. He filled their heart with wisdom, and showed them both good and evil. He set His eye upon their hearts to show them the greatness of His works…that they might glory in His wondrous acts. Moreover, He gave them instructions and the law of life for an inheritance. He made an everlasting covenant with them. And their eye saw the majesty of His glory and their ears heard His glorious voice, and He said to them: Beware of all iniquity."[2]

Could He have given them more? Knowing the temptation that was coming, He protected them with every needful gift of nature and of grace. Why seek for knowledge by eating of the forbidden tree when God Himself, by the reflection of His law in conscience, "showed them both good and evil," so far as this was necessary for them?

"Moreover," and here come in the protecting commandments, "He gave them the law of life for an inheritance and an everlasting covenant with Him."

Is there the faintest sign that He grudged them anything? He would have His Commandments regarded,

---

1 Gen. 2:8, 9, 15, 17   2 Eccles. 17:5, *et seq.*

not as restriction, but as protection; not as curtailing liberty, but as guarding it; not as bondage, but as an inheritance to be prized. Yet at Satan's suggestion that any limitation was a grievance—"Why not eat of every tree?; your eyes shall be opened and you shall be as gods"—through curiosity, just to see what would happen, they fell from their trust in God, from their loyalty to Him who had given them all!

This was the first temptation—to think God hard; that He was withholding what would have made them higher and happier. Does the subtle serpent ever try the same deception upon us?

"But all this is the very oldest of old stories. It has no bearing on the world of today. It is not interesting."

"No bearing"! Why, it is the most up-to-date of all topics, discussed in the columns of the daily papers by the side of golf, channel-swimming, the latest casualties in the air, prize-fighting, greyhound racing, and other engrossing subjects.

"Not interesting, Though it goes to the root of all that most nearly concerns us. That "Why?" of Satan in the "garden of pleasure" is the sum and substance of all the problems that are agitating the minds of men at this moment: "Why these restrictions on our liberty?" men, women, and children are crying. "Why may I not think and speak and act as I like—eat of every tree in the garden of pleasure, read every book, see every film, run every risk?" "Die the death"! there is no death. The days of magic and superstition, our leaders tell us, are past. There are no terrors beyond the grave. From the beasts we came, and our life will go out like theirs. "For we are born of nothing, and after this we shall be as if we had not been...our body shall be ashes, and our spirit shall be poured abroad as soft air.... Come, therefore, and let us enjoy the good things that are present.... Let us crown ourselves with roses before they be withered. Let no meadow escape our riot. Let none of us go without his part in luxury...for this is our portion and our lot!"[1]

Can we say there is no parallel here to the speech of our morning papers?

The first chapters of Genesis dealing with Creation must go today, condemned by "the final word of Science." Tomorrow it will be Exodus and the Commandments. The bulwarks that protect Christianity and civilisation are giving way on every side. Only the warning finger of the Church is upheld. Only her hand protects the Scriptures. Her voice is coming to be the only one to speak with no uncertain sound, to echo clearly the Voice of Sinai: "Thou shalt not!"

Who can say that these words of God in the beginning have no relation with the present time? The Church judges differently. Every year, in the stillness of Holy Saturday, when the awful price of our Redemption has been paid, and all is quiet round the Sepulchre, she gathers her children round her to review the history of mankind from the beginning. She does not find it superfluous or uninteresting to remind us that God created man to His own image, and set him in the garden of pleasure, not to run riot there, but to "dress it and keep it" by fidelity to Him who gave it as a test. The lesson it teaches is as necessary to the safety of the world

---

[1] Wis. 2:2, *et seq.*

now as it was then—to use the creatures of God so far as they help to the attainment of His designs, to abstain from them when they would hinder. The Home of this twentieth century needs it; the League of Nations needs it; the very foundations of society need it for problems which defy all solutions that leave God out of count.

The lessons of God's inspired Word are always pertinent, and the Church hands them down reverently to all time for the healing of the nations. Ever young, she falls in with the spirit and needs of every age. She, too, brings out of her treasury things new and old. She has her new festivals. She has her moving pictures. Swiftly and vividly as her year goes on, they pass before us as present. To her, time is but a point. "This is the night," she says, "in which our forefathers, the children of Israel, passed through the Red Sea on dry foot.... This is the night which alone deserved to know the time and hour in which Christ rose again from the grave.... Wonderfully created, more wonderfully redeemed, may we," she prays, "resist with strong mind the allurements of sin, that we may deserve to arrive at eternal joys."

So our little Spanish theologian was not so wide of the mark in asserting that the Sign of the Cross—obedience and sacrifice—would have discomfited the serpent and left paradise unfallen!

II

Trust in God—Repairer

"O strange vineyard!"—Jer. 2:21

How frail we proved at our best! How ready, for a selfish gratification, to surrender our loyalty to God!

With all their light and grace, those two in Eden might have been thought beyond the reach of temptation. Yet at the first test they failed, as Satan thought, irretrievably. "Thou art wounded as well as we; thou art become like unto us," was his cruel taunt. And—"a murderer from the beginning," as our Lord calls him—he waited impatiently for the sequel.

Yet what a knowledge of God our very frailty brought! What revelation of His character and perfections! Little did the tempter suspect the mercy in store for the race that was to number among its members the Son of God made Man! Instead of punishment, swift, terrible and eternal, there was compassion. The sin of Adam and Eve was less than that of the nobler, keener spirits which had fallen.

And God had pity. He had loved them from eternity. He had set His eye upon their hearts.[1] He knew that they must be forever happy with Him or miserable without Him. He could not let them go. Man should be, not forgiven only, but restored and raised to a height of which the rebel angels had never dreamed. A Saviour must be found for him.

And the Eternal Son said: *"Behold I come!"*

"O felix culpa!" the Church exclaims in a rapture of admiration and gratitude.... Do *we* take it as a matter of course? Except once a year—perhaps—when, following her lead, we pass swiftly over the world's history from the beginning, do we ever think of the incomprehensible forbearance of God when—bold as children from very terror—the culprits stood accusing each other before Him?

Are we not inclined to pass over with little thought the wonderful transition—as it seems to us—from justice to mercy, from the threat: "In what day soever thou shalt eat of it thou shalt die the death," to: "I will put enmities between thee and the woman...and she shall crush thy head"?

We sympathise with our first parents as, weeping and wailing, they exchanged the "paradise of pleasure" for the barren earth outside. Like them, we are sorry beyond measure *for ourselves* and keenly deplore the evils they have brought *upon us*. We concentrate upon the loss of Eden, on the thorns and thistles, on labour and toil. But do we take to heart as we should the wrong done to Him who "touched inwardly with sorrow of heart, repented him that he had made man"?[2]

---

1 Eccles. 17:7
2 Gen. 6:6

To see things as God sees them is the only true point of view. Should it not be the only point for His intelligent creatures? Seeing sin, whether in himself or in others, as it affects God, a loyal subject, a child devoted to his Father's interests, cannot but be touched inwardly with sorrow of heart. To this we shall come when life is done. It will be the instantaneous revelation of the Particular Judgment:

> "The sight of Him will kindle in thy heart
> All tender, gracious, reverential thoughts.
> Thou wilt be sick with love, and yearn for Him,
> And feel as though thou couldst but pity Him,
> That one so sweet should e'er have placed Himself
> At disadvantage such, as to be used
> So vilely by a being so vile as thee...."[1]

Cast out of Eden, Adam and Eve have every claim upon our compassion. But let us think at least as much of the mercy shown them as of their pain. The heavenly Paradise was still kept open to them. They would "die the death," but not "the second death." Amid the thorns and the thistles, the labour and the toil of their nine hundred years' penance, their All-merciful Father was waiting to cheer them and their children with the continually renewed Promise that was to make over to them immeasurably more than they had lost.

Meantime mankind fell away rapidly from the knowledge of God and the observance of the Natural Law. Idolatry, foul and cruel, took the place of loving worship and trust. Men came to adore what they instinctively loathed and feared.

---
1 "Dream of Gerontius," Cardinal Newman.

Even the Chosen People, protected by continual miracles, showed little gratitude and trust. The Divine Patience, in bearing with their perpetual murmuring and prevarication, is among the most touching revelations to us of the character of God.

Sustained by type and prophecy, belief in the Redeemer to come strengthened with every generation. His race, family, characteristics, the chief circumstances of His life and death, were gradually disclosed, now in the inspired words of Scripture, now in the mysterious utterances of a Sibyl, or stammering oracle, so that, as time went on, even the Gentile world came to look to the Hebrew people for the Messiah of universal expectation.

What is the history of this strange race but the record of a Divine bid for a nation's loyalty and trust, the story of a Covenant revealing on one side a marvellous persistence of fidelity and protection, and on the other—for the most part—a heartless insensibility?

Freed by a series of miraculous interventions from a cruel slavery, they revolted against their leaders and planned a return to captivity. Divinely led during forty years by a pillar of cloud or fire, they grumbled at every provision for them by the way. Fed daily with bread from heaven—an army of six hundred thousand fighting men, with their families, they pined for the flesh-pots of Egypt. With God to fight for them and give them victory, they clamoured for a king to lead them to battle, and amid the lightning and thunders of Sinai, danced in thanksgiving round the golden calf that had brought them out of bondage!

And for fifteen hundred years the patience of God bore with them. Despising alike His favours, His threats, and His chastisements, killing the prophets sent to warn and instruct them, they remained the people of His predilection by whom the world was to receive its promised Saviour.

At times, indeed, we hear a Divine plaint:

"Shall two walk together except they be agreed?"[1]

"Put me in remembrance and let us plead together. Tell me if thou hast anything to justify thyself."[2]

"What iniquity have your fathers found in me that they are gone far from me?"[3]

"What is there that I ought to do more to my vineyard that I have not done to it? I looked that it should bring forth grapes and it hath brought forth wild grapes."[4]

"Yet I planted thee a chosen vineyard, all true seed; how then art thou turned unto me into that which is good for nothing, O strange vineyard?"[5]

With Divine generosity God complains of the injury His people do themselves rather than of the wrong done to Him:

"Be astonished, O ye heavens, at this, and be very desolate, saith the Lord. For my people have done two evils. They have forsaken me, the fountain of living water, and have digged to themselves cisterns, broken cisterns that can hold no water."[6]

---

1 Amos 3:3   2 Isaias 43:26   3 Jer. 2:5
4 Isaias 5:4   5 Jer. 2:21   6 Jer. 2:12, 13

"O that thou hadst hearkened to my commandments: thy peace had been as a river, and thy justice as the waves of the sea."[1]

"Thou hast broken my yoke…thou hast said: I will not serve."[2]

"Know thou and see that it is an evil and a bitter thing for thee to have left the Lord thy God."[3]

"Return, you rebellious children, and I will heal your rebellions.… Return and I will not turn away my face from you, and I will not be angry for ever."

As captives or as teachers—one day a doomed race, hated, feared, and persecuted; the next, sharing the throne of their conquerors, their sacred writings reverently studied and laid up amhoongst the world's most treasured lore; enlightening and leavening the four great Empires through which they passed, so they moved through two thousand years, moulding under Divine guidance the destinies of the nations under whose sway they came, and all with a view to the Desired of all nations who was on His way. The time of His Advent was made known to Daniel because he was "a man of desires." But it was for a child of despised Nazareth to draw him to earth at last.

"Afterwards He was seen upon earth and conversed with men."[4] The fullness of time had come. "And the Word was made Flesh, and dwelt amongst us."

---

[1] Isaias 48:18 [2] Jer. 2:20 [3] Jer. 2:19
[4] Bar. 3:38

III

Trust in God—Redeemer

"In the face of Christ Jesus."—II Cor. 4:6.

MAY WE NOT say that in all His relations with us the main design of our Heavenly Father seems to be to invite our trust? He will have us from the first to call Him "Father," the most endearing of names for all it suggests and implies—solicitude, tenderness, prevision, provision, indulgence…and on our side loving obedience and trust. "Is not He thy father that hath possessed thee, and made thee, and created thee?"[1]

When, through the perversity of mankind, the ideal of fatherhood in God was almost obliterated, He came Himself to restore it. The Incarnation of God the Son renewed the face of the earth, not only by the Sacrifice that redeemed us, but by those three years of familiar friendship which, revealing in His own Person the character of the Father, won back for Him the trust that was all but lost on earth.

Even under the Old Dispensation, so tender was His provision for His people, so vigilant His care, that He could

---
1 Deut. 32:6

challenge them to find anything wanting. "What more could I have done?" he asked.

Yes, there was one thing more: "Show me Thy Face!" It is the babe's need at its mother's breast. Even there it must see her face to be content. Hide and seek is their first game together. A moment's hiding means a piteous cry. In her face it reads all it needs to learn. It is the foundation of its love and trust, because it is the revelation of herself. We never outgrow that instinct. We crave for the face of our absent friend. In various ways his words may reach us, but they do not satisfy.

He who made the human heart knows its inmost need. The cry: "Show me Thy Face!" is His inspiration. But how is it to be answered, since no one hath seen the Face of God at any time? Who but Himself could have found a solution? Angels would have told us we must wait for the Beatific Vision. But we need it here and now: a human face to be, as to one another, the foundation of our love and trust.

St. Paul tells us where we are to seek and find it. "In the face of Christ Jesus." So, in the Third Mass for Christmas Day, the Church, leading us from types to their realization says that "God who many ways spake in times past to the fathers by the prophets, last of all hath spoken to us by His Son." He is "the brightness of His glory and the figure of His substance;"[1] we have the light of the knowledge of God *in the face of Christ Jesus.*

Those who looked into that Face understood these words. Not only by blotting out on the cross the handwriting

---
1   Heb. 1:3

that stood against us, but through the intimacy of daily intercourse, would the Son of Man restore the loving relations between God and man. "The Word was made Flesh and dwelt amongst us," says St. John. And as if striving vainly to express in human speech his amazement at the Divine condescension, he goes on exultingly: "that which was from the beginning, which we have heard, which we have seen with our eyes, which we have looked upon and our hands have handled…which was with the Father and hath appeared to us, we have seen, and do bear witness and declare unto you."[1] "….all the time that the Lord Jesus came in and went out amongst us," says St. Peter, in like bewilderment at the intercourse to which they were admitted. And not they only, but all comers:

"Healing all manner of sickness and every infirmity," winning, by the blending of majesty and gentleness in His Person and His ways, by His heavenly doctrine and astounding miracles, all whom pride and jealousy had not estranged, He went about Judea and Galilee. The crowds that pressed upon Him from morning till night—publicans and sinners, the sick and the little children, the poor and the down-trodden, knew Him as their Friend. They knew Him to be wholly at their service, ready at a moment's notice to interrupt His teaching and go wherever His sympathy and help were needed. The touch of His hand, the tones of His voice, thousands knew. The lepers, the possessed, the outcasts of society, shunned and despised by all, were none of them beyond the reach of His compassion. To identify Himself with His human

---
1   1 John 1:1, 2

brethren, to make Himself one of us, to accept the love and trust He inspired, that so He might reveal to us the Father, this was the desire of His heart, the goal of all His labour and sufferings.

When His heart is fullest, it is of the Father that He speaks. It is to the Father that He draws attention:

"The Father knoweth Me and I know the Father."

"No one knoweth the Father but the Son, and he to whom it shall please the Son to reveal Him."

"I know Him because I am from Him."

"I and the Father are one."

"All things whatsoever the Father hath are Mine."

And He would share all with us His brethren:

"Whatsoever I have heard of My Father, I have made known to you."

"I came forth from the Father and am come into the world."

"The hour cometh when I will show you plainly of the Father."

"I say not to you that I will ask the Father for you, for the Father Himself loveth you, because you have loved Me."

When at the Last Supper one of the disciples asks Him to show them the Father, He answers, as if disappointed: "So long have I been with you and have you not known Me? Philip, he that seeth Me seeth the Father also. How sayest thou 'Show us the Father?' Do you not believe that I am in the Father and the Father in Me?"

"Whatsoever you shall ask the Father in My name, that

will I do, that the Father may be glorified in the Son."

"I ascend to My Father and to your Father, to My God and to your God."

Has He not given us grounds for trust?

It was His custom to elicit a profession of faith or trust from those He was about to heal, even to make such profession a condition of the cure:

"If Thou canst do anything, help us, having compassion on us," said the father of the lunatic boy:

"If thou canst believe," replied our Lord at once, "all things are possible to him that believeth."

As if mistrust actually tied His hands, we are told: "He could not do many miracles there because of their unbelief." Trust in Him was His first lesson to the multitudes—men, women and children that flocked after Him into the desert, regardless of shelter, food, business or rest, so they might hang about Him, hear the sound of His voice, look upon His face. Trust was His first lesson to those He called to forsake all and follow Him.

At times He asked people to do what seemed a foolish thing, just to see if they would trust Him. The lepers to whom He said: "Go, show yourselves to the priests," might have answered: "What good can they do? they have never cured anyone!" But they went and were healed on the way.

It would seem as if to trust He can refuse nothing. Wherever He finds it, among heathens, Jews, or Christians, it is all-powerful with Him. Forgiveness and miracles it wins with ease. Those who excel in trust He deigns to call His friends.

On the other hand, in presence of unbelief, we hear of Him "sighing deeply: 'O unbelieving and perverse generation, how long shall I be with you, how long shall I suffer you!' " And because the very act of faith must be His prompting. He comes to the help of the petitioner, showing Himself as anxious to give as they are to ask. To two blind men He says:

"Do you believe that I can do this unto you?"

"Yea, Lord."

"According to your faith be it done unto you."

A leper comes to Him:

"Lord, if Thou wilt, Thou canst make me clean."

"I will; be thou made clean."

To Jairus, whose little daughter has just died, the answer follows quickly on his prayer for help, as if doubt or mistrust might supervene:

"Fear not, believe only and she shall be safe."

In the synagogue where He was teaching on the sabbath was a poor sufferer who had "a spirit of infirmity eighteen years and was bowed together, neither could she look upwards at all. Whom when Jesus saw He called her unto Him and said to her: 'Woman, thou art delivered from thy infirmity.' And He laid His hands upon her, and immediately she was made straight and glorified God."

It was all so grandly and gently done. On the Sabbath, knowing He would draw upon Himself the anger of the ruler of the synagogue. Unasked, except by His own pitying Heart and healing hands that longed to help. With tender words—"thou art delivered"—not from thy deformity, in

His eyes it was "infirmity" only. With loving action; He laid His hands upon her, "no pain, no suspense": immediately she was made straight and, kneeling at His feet, was looking into His face, glorifying God.

But—note the terrible change:

Among the things which touched to the quick His sensitive Heart were cruelty to the suffering poor, hypocrisy, misleading of the people, and, above all, disloyalty to His Father and to the Holy Spirit by the rejection of the known truth. All these He found here in Satan and his accomplice:

"And the ruler of the synagogue being angry that Jesus had healed on the sabbath, said to the multitude: 'Six days there are wherein you ought to work. In them therefore come and be healed, and not on the sabbath-day.'"

"And the Lord, answering him, said: ' Ye hypocrites, doth not every one of you on the sabbath day loose his ox or his ass from the manger and lead them to water? And ought not this daughter of Abraham, whom Satan hath bound, lo, these eighteen years, be loosed from this bond on the sabbath day?' And when He said these things all His adversaries were ashamed; and all the people rejoiced for all the things that were gloriously done by Him."

How that terrible anger, no less than His gentle compassion, must have confirmed the faith of the apostles and of the simple-minded worshippers there, revealing to them the Divine Perfections of Mercy and Justice—"in the Face of Christ Jesus!"

"This daughter of Abraham," our Lord called the poor sufferer who with such humility and fortitude had persevered in the service of God. There is no great merit in trust until it is tested. Tried, as it seems to us at times, almost to the breaking point, it becomes heroic and is all-powerful with God. Such was the faith or trust of Abraham— "our father Abraham," our Lady calls him—and the Church in her daily sacrifice. Would it not be disgraceful if such heroism in the father should prove no spur to the children!

Faith, Hope and Charity—the three theological virtues which unite the soul immediately with God—are all contained in trust. It glorifies all the Divine Perfections, which throughout the Holy Scriptures He reveals to us as grounds for our trust. He promises, He threatens, He insists, as if to trust Him were to do Him a signal service. "Let them trust in Thee who know Thee,"[1] says the Church. "Let me know Thee and know myself," says St. Augustine— the mountain and the grain of sand at its base. The two go together, and both teach the same lesson—TRUST.

---

1   Gradual for Septuagesima Sunday

IV

Trust in His Omnipotence

"I believe in God the Father Almighty, Maker of heaven and earth, and of all things visible and invisible."—Nicene Creed.

I LOOK UP at midnight into the heavens studded with stars, and think what Creator and creation mean. All this vast universe sprang into existence at the word of God. With a word He could destroy it and bring into being, not merely another such universe, but myriads, differing from each other in every particular, with mysteries, laws, furniture beyond our possibilities of conception. And this He could do indefinitely through endless ages without the least diminution of His resources. What adoration is due to Omnipotence such as this!

Father Faber says somewhere that a child's first sight of the ocean is an epoch in its life. Its idea of God will be different once it has seen the sea. What, then, must be the revelation of God to a thoughtful traveller out on the boundless ocean at night, or to the astronomer on the mountain summit under the starry sky!

Yet there are so-called scientists and thoughtless sightseers whom neither mind nor sense draws to the stupendous works of the Creator; men of whom St. Paul said in his day that "the wrath of God is revealed from heaven against their ungodliness and injustice.... For the invisible things of Him from the creation of the world are clearly seen, being understood by the things that are made; His eternal power also and divinity; so that they are inexcusable. Because that when they knew God they have not glorified him as God or given thanks; but became vain in their thoughts and their foolish heart was darkened. For professing themselves wise they became fools.[1]" Is this less true today?

The disclosures of science are but opening the door into deeper and unsuspected mysteries, so that we wonder what the world of a hundred years hence will be like if it lasts so long, and shudder at the possibilities which a future war may reveal. It is being said that in proportion to his mastery of the forces of nature is man losing power over himself. Are we able to deny this? In any case, the words of our Lord are being more than ever verified: "He that is not with Me is against Me and he that gathereth not with Me scattereth." Is the knowledge of God and of Christ our Lord, which in the Bible is cast upon every shore, shown in the relations of Christian nations with those whom they call brethren? Or are the heathen being taught vices and horrors unknown till now?

Time after time does Scripture repeat that man was created in the image and likeness of God, chiefly by the gifts of understanding and free-will which are the reflection of His Wisdom and Omnipotence and the foundation of His

---

1 1 Rom. 1:18,22

other gifts to us. They are above all the manifestation of His liberality and confidence. He will not be served by slaves. Those who are to serve Him in this world and to be happy with Him forever in the next are to be His willing servants and "most dear children." They are to have the happiness of their eternity immeasurably increased by their cooperation with Him in the work of their salvation. To this end He gives them the grand but dread power of free-will. "God made man from the beginning and left him in the hand of his own counsel. He added His commandments and precepts. If thou wilt keep His commandments…they shall preserve thee."

This power of free-will God Himself deigns to respect. He will give abundant grace to aid and strengthen, but He will not coerce it. "Because Thou art Lord of all Thou makest Thyself gracious to all…and with great reverence Thou disposest of us." Wonderful words in the mouth of the Creator and the Omnipotent! How can men be so depraved and so foolish as, not only to abuse, but to disclaim this magnificent gift, or to take it amiss that they were not consulted as to its bestowal!

They would have us welcome as a grand discovery the final teaching of Science, that our ancestors were apes; that "man's brain has been evolved from that of an anthropoid ape, and that in the process no new structure has been introduced, and no new or strange faculty interpolated."[1]

Such statements seem to deny in man the existence of the soul—his free-will, therefore, and responsibility for his actions. Like the beasts which serve him, he passes away

---
1 Sir Arthur Keith's Presidential Address to The British Association

without hope or fear of a future state since there is nothing beyond this life to deserve punishment or reward.

The boys of Westminster School attending divine service for the first time after the vacation were invited from the pulpit of Westminster Abbey by an Anglican Bishop[1] to "share the contempt of men of science for the ignorance, magic and fear of the men who desire to preserve old errors." Choosing for his text the words of St. Paul: "Walk as children of light," the preacher assured his young hearers that "certain statements of St. Paul…cannot be reconciled with the findings of science"; that there is a sharp conflict between Science and Religion, and that honest people must side with the "men of science to whom the quest of truth is one of life's greatest joys."

Thus are our English boys—presumably Christians—warned within the venerable walls of Westminster Abbey against "clinging to the old faith." In this way are they being prepared for life here and hereafter as husbands, fathers, citizens—servants and children of God.

What a shock must such words have been—if not to the lads themselves—at least to their parents! The education of their children, to be worthy of the name, must aim at fitting them not only to grow up useful citizens, but by the observance of God's commandments to lead Christian lives and prepare themselves for the life of the world to come. They came to the venerable Abbey to hear the Christian faith shaken to its foundations. For the teaching of the sermon was a virtual denial of the existence of the soul. Refusing to others the exercise

---

1 Dr. Benras

of private judgment which he claimed for himself, the Bishop would have the boys accept his word in place of the traditional teaching of Christianity which can no longer be harmonized with science.

According to the President of the British Association the soul of the brute and the soul of the man differ only in degree, not in kind, for he insists that in the process of brain evolution from the ape's to the man's no new or strange faculty has been introduced.

This is rank materialism. The difference between the living principle of the human and that of the brute creation is not in degree only, but in kind. "The soul of man performs purely spiritual acts; it forms mental concepts and expresses them in articulate language; it recognizes moral responsibility; it has the power of choice…it invents; it creates. This is beyond the capacity of any monkey's brain, however developed."[1] Scripture and the Catholic Church teach that it is the direct action of God breathing into the living soul the spirit endowed with the glorious prerogatives of understanding and free-will that makes the difference.

As children of the Church we look to her to tell us what we may, what we must, and what we must not hold as to the vexed questions of the day. She who has been accused of keeping the Scriptures from the people is now the sole effectual guardian of God's inspired Word. And at this momentous crisis she bids us turn to the first chapters of Genesis and read:

---

1 *The Month*, October 1927, p. 347. Fr. Keating, S.J., "Where does Adam come in?"

"And God said: Let us make man to our own image and likeness."[1] And again: "In the day that God created man, He made him to the likeness of God."[2] And yet again: "And the Lord God formed man of the slime of the earth and breathed into his face the breath of life and man became a living soul."[3]

> Note: The Biblical Commission states the authoritative attitude of the Church on the general and particular criticisms of so-called scientists against the traditional account of the creation of man, and the objectivity of the scriptural record.
>
> Summed up, the Commission asserts that the first three chapters of *Genesis* are wholly historical in character and partly figurative in form; that any system which denies the historical character of these chapters is false; that the facts related which affect the foundation of the Christian faith cannot be questioned; that every word and phrase need not be taken according to its literal meaning; that the natural sciences are not included in the divine communication, and that the word "day" (distinguishing the six days of creation) is open to discussion.
>
> The Pope in 1909 confirmed these decisions of the Biblical Commission and ordered their publication.
>
> We may hold that in the use of allegory and symbol the sacred writer accommodated himself to the mentality of his public and used the language of his time. Recording the sternest facts of history, men have at all times employed every kind of figurative expression. Some of the finest narrations of objective historical episodes belong to this class of literature.

---

1 Gen. 1:26
2 Gen. 5:1
3 Gen. 2:7

We are not allowed to call into question the literal and historical meaning when in these chapters it is a question of the narration of facts which touch the foundations of the Christian religion, as, for example, the creation of all things in the beginning of time; the particular creation of man; the unity of the human race; the original happiness of our first parents in a state of justice, integrity and immortality; the divine command laid upon man for the proving of his obedience; the transgression of that divine command at the instigation of the devil under the form of a serpent; the fall of our first parents from their primitive state of innocence; and the promise of a future Redeemer....

These decisions of the Biblical Commission provide us with our fixed beliefs and open points, by giving us the safeguard of an authoritative and ecclesiastical guidance."

(cf. "The Biblical Commission and *Genesis*," The *Catholic Gazette*, Dec. 1927. J. Hogan.)

What more do we need to know? Is it not more to our purpose to inquire what is to become of us in the unending life to come, than what was the possible origin of our forefathers some ages back in the world's history? Weary with modern theories we turn to God's inspired Word which sufficed for our forefathers in days of simpler faith, and deeper minds, and *nobler instincts.*

"Knowledge puffeth up," says St. Paul. Yet not all knowledge has so baneful a result, for true "knowledge is a fountain of life to him that possesseth it." The highest intellects are the humblest and the clearest because the truest. Lucifer fell from heaven because—our Lord tells us—"the truth is not in him." The knowledge that puffs up is the self-sufficiency which, relying on its own "discoveries," disdains the possibility of error. The true scientist, conscious of his own limitations, and of the enormous fields of speculation yet unexplored, is humble and ready to learn. He does not presume to give as the result of his labours and through his own lips the final word of Science. He finds the convictions of yesterday superseded by those of today, which in their turn may have to give place to the facts of tomorrow.

Now, as never before, we are told, men demand that Science should be humble-minded. Questions "settled for all time" are not common among leaders of scientific thought today.

We may hold to evolution up to a certain point. That there has been some evolution is probable. There are people who think it may have been downward and not upward, and that man after the Fall degenerated rapidly. But the whole matter is mere speculation, not demonstrated fact. The unsolved difficulty for the evolutionist is the absence of the missing links between the species. Whether the final word of science will ever be spoken makes no difference to Catholic doctrine. Evolution is only a modern way of solving the riddle of the material universe. It does not explain how the brain of man, which has given him his powers of understanding, speaking, learning, has come into being. Sir A. Keith insists—and this is what chiefly affects the question of brain evolution—that there has been no introduction of any new or spiritual element.

Theories have their day—and pass. Our thoughts go forward to a day when speculations as to our forefathers will give place to a reality that concerns ourselves; when this word will be in the mouth of all men: "Thou art just, O Lord, and Thy judgment is right… The judgments of the Lord are true, justified in themselves."

God has a place in this world and in the next for every one of us, a place for which our service to Him here is to prepare us. As a rule His action in His own world is quiet and unobtrusive. Yet He has not left Himself without witness, or His intelligent creatures without light and knowledge of His Will. In what concerns their belief and practice, He says to them: "Hear the Church."

Our time here is too short for fruitless speculation: "What signifies," says à Kempis, "making a great dispute about abstruse matters, for not knowing of which we shall not be questioned at the day of judgment…. We shall not be examined what we have read, but what we have done."

I believe that when the eternal design has reached fulfillment, when "all things are ready," the world on which I stand will pass away, all its glory reduced to ashes. At the summons: "Arise, ye dead, and come to judgment," the whole human race in the twinkling of an eye[1] will rise from the grave and be gathered together for the final act in the world's history. Creation will be in wild disarray, the heavens passing away with great violence, the elements melting with the burning heat.[2] But there those innumerable millions, in bodies now indestructible, will stand, awaiting the coming of the Judge.

---

1 1 Cor. 15:52   2 2 Peter 3:10

I shall be there. All whom I have known in life, or from hearsay or history, will be there, our personal identity remaining intact. Yet we shall be changed, says St. Paul. How? Is the secret of Divine Omnipotence? And changed to what? That depends on the use we shall have made of the free-will God has given us which He will never coerce: "Before man is life and death, good and evil, that which he shall choose shall be given him."[1] On his choice as fixed in the moment of death eternity will depend. If through God›s mercy we die in His grace, our change at the Resurrection will mean eternal Life; to die unsanctified by that grace is "the second death."

How we must prize and dread the free-will on which so much depends—that by its co-operation with God will secure our eternal salvation, or, on the other hand, by resistance to His Will can defeat His designs for us!

His Omnipotence alone would not reassure us in our fears. We need a father's ear, a father's heart. So from the beginning He has declared Himself, not Creator only, but Father: "Is not He thy father that hath possessed thee, and made thee, and created thee?"

A little child, going out to work or play, runs with its treasured toy to its mother and lays it in her lap, saying: "Save that for me!" Will she lose sight of it or forget it?

O God, my Father, I hasten to Thee with Thy grand gift to me on which my All depends! I dare not trust it to other hands, least of all to my own. Save it for me. Only in Thy keeping can my free will be safe. Save it from itself. Save it from the perils of this life and bring it at last to the

---
1 Eccles. 15:18

security of the Home Thou hast prepared for those who put their trust in Thee.

V

Trust in His Fatherhood

"I will be his father and he shall be my son."—Apoc. 21:7

THE HEIR to a throne may be excused, perhaps, for over-rating his privileges. He stands on a giddy height and careful instruction as to the limits of the royal prerogative will be necessary if trouble later is to be avoided.

Thanks to our Baptism, we are all royal children; by adoption, indeed, but one that carries with it the rights of sonship. Our position has its dangers. The dignity to which we are raised can never be over-estimated, but its privileges may be forfeited through our failure to realise them. How many of us take the trouble to consider what this adoption means and entails?

That "we should be called and should be the sons of God" implies a love for us so astounding as to be almost incredible. We know that it is the nature of goodness to communicate itself. But has not the Eternal Father a Son of infinite perfection, equal to Himself? Why should He seek to include in the Divine Family such despicable little creatures as we are and make us sharers in the complacency with which He regards the Son of His Love?

We can never hear without amazement St. Peter's words: "Partakers of the Divine Nature." For what can such words mean? We know of ambition among angels so inexplicable as to aim at the Throne of God Himself: "I will be like the Most High!" We know of ambition on earth so selfish as to wade through the blood of nearest and dearest to keep a throne for itself alone. But in God we find love so incomprehensible as to raise creatures—rebellious creatures—to the dignity of sons and heirs, "Heirs indeed of God and joint heirs with Christ."

To give any idea of the height to which we are lifted by this adoption—that "we should be called and should be the sons of God,"[1] is an impossibility. Whatever else God has done for us or will do for us is less than this gift of sonship.

It seems a simple thing to stand beside a font and watch a baptism.... Oh, that we could see the admiration of the angels flocking round. For what do they behold? This child has suddenly received a new life, a re-birth. It has been spiritually begotten by God. From being a servant it has been received into His family. How do the Princes of Heaven listen to the solemn charge of the Church: "Receive this white garment and see thou carry it without stain before the judgment seat of our Lord Jesus Christ that thou mayest have eternal life."

The Old and the New Testaments vie with each other in tenderness of expression for the adopted children: "With

---
[1] 1 John 3:1

what circumspection hast Thou judged Thy own children, Thy children, O Lord, whom Thou lovest."[1] "For Thou didst admonish and try them as a father."[2] "O children of Israel, fight not against the Lord…for it is not good for you."[3] "Is not He thy Father that hath possessed thee, and made thee, and created thee?"[4] "He will have mercy on thee more than a mother."[5]

The Son of God has come on earth to translate the Father to us; to give us the trust of children in Him; to be our advocate with Him. And this is how He speaks to us:

"Fear not, little flock. Let not your heart be troubled, nor let it be afraid. I will not leave you orphans. I have not called you servants, but friends, brethren, little children. For the Father Himself loveth you.… My Father and your Father, My God and your God."

In both Testaments it is the same Spirit that speaks, the Spirit of the Father and the Son, He who has been called "What is sweetest in God." "O how good and sweet is Thy Spirit, O Lord!"[6] Tender and winning are these incentives to confidence, the bid that He, the Lord of all things, makes for our trust. The God of the Old Testament has been called hard. Do His own words reveal hardness? When the English people were robbed by their rulers of the Sacraments which for a thousand years had been to them sources of life and strength, God left them the Scriptures to sustain what measure of faith and hope they still retained. That, too, is failing now. Will He restore to England all she has lost by giving back to her the Faith for

---

1 Wis. 12:21   2 Wis. 11:2   3 2 Par. 13:12
4 Deut. 32:6   5 Eccles. 4:11   6 Wis. 12:1

which her martyrs died, with the treasures which are only safe in the keeping of His Church?

But do we, the children of the Church, make the use of the Holy Scriptures that we might? Do we turn to them for the light and the consolation they are meant to give, and do give to those who, following the lead of the Church, know them by experience to be "a strong defence"?

What strength and comfort are stored for us in those names of Truth itself, "Father, sons, heirs"! For the words of God are not as ours. They effect what they express. He is a real Father, easy to get on with, indulgent, kind. Sons and heirs look for indulgence. If the name of Judge frightens us, we have those reassuring words: "With what circumspection hast Thou judged *Thy own children.*"

All that concerns us as to soul and body—our home and its circumstances, our health and strength or weakness and pain, our occupations and relations with others, down to the smallest details of daily life, our varied experiences and the way in which our will reacts upon them—all this is the loving concern of our Father who is in heaven. He loves us each and all incomparably more than the tenderest of fathers loves his child. "For Thou lovest all things that are and hatest none of the things which Thou hast made, for Thou didst not make anything, hating it."[1]

"Why did God make you?" said a priest to a little child.
"Because He loved me."
"And how do you know He loves you?"

---

1 Wis. 11:25

"Because He made me. If He hadn't loved me He needn't have made me."

It is the father's office to cherish and to comfort, to protect and to provide. All this our Heavenly Father does for His children with a solicitude to which the fatherhood of earth affords no parallel. Scripture sums it up in the word Providence: "Thy Providence, O Father, governs it." To govern is to direct to a determined end. But so gentle and unobtrusive is the action of Divine Providence, so disguised under the laws of Nature as to be practically identified with them in the minds of men. Yet these laws are Its servants always, and at times It asserts Its independence. The faithful, no whit surprised, speak of miracle, whilst sceptics refuse to acknowledge any intervention even when this is unmistakable.

How inconsistent we are in our conceptions of God and in our judgment of His dealings with us. If He obtrudes Himself on our notice and puts forward His claims, we find Him aggressive. If He conceals Himself and His action behind the laws of Nature and everyday occurrences, we either ignore Him altogether and patch together theories to account for anything out of the ordinary, or we blame Him for not asserting Himself so manifestly as to save us the humiliation of faith and trust.

Certainly, the gentle action of His Providence in human affairs and in the government of the universe does lay Him open to the charge of unobtrusiveness. Yet He will not be altogether ignored. If men thrust Him aside or defy His authority, He may wait awhile, but sooner or later He will step in and vindicate His rights.

In how many an unforeseen peril or unguarded moment, at times of crisis when a false step would have spoilt our lives, His Providence has been at hand to intervene and save us! We must beware of attributing to chance the events of life, whether great or small: "Thou art my God, my lots are in Thy hands."[1] "Lots are cast into the lap, but they are disposed of by the Lord."[2]

He would have us diligent servants and faithful stewards in the trusts confided to us. Yet not "solicitous," that is, not over anxious as to the result of our endeavours, as if we laboured alone, without His help and blessing. "Do not look forward," says St. Francis de Sales, "to what may happen tomorrow. The same everlasting Father who cares for you today will care for you tomorrow and every day. Either He will shield you from suffering or give you unfailing strength to bear it. Be at peace, then, and put aside all anxious thoughts and imaginations."

> "O Lord, how happy should we be
> If we could cast our care on Thee;
>   If we from self could rest;
> And feel at heart that One above,
> In perfect wisdom, perfect love
>   Is working for the best."[3]

The lives of the servants of God are one continuous proof of His delight in their trust: "Fear not, little flock," He says, as time after time He comes to their help, even by miracle. One who knew by experience the horrors and

---

1 Ps. 30:16   2 Prov. 16:33   3 Keble

hardships of penal times used to say: "It very ill becomes the servants of God to be faint hearted, for they know well that God is Omnipotent and that He loves them infinitely, and therefore will permit nothing that could hurt them." When her designs were opposed she gave herself wholly into God's hands and said it was He must answer for her, and then—"rested herself in God."[1]

"Commit thy way to the Lord and trust in Him."[2]

"He that is mounted upon the heaven is thy helper and underneath are the everlasting arms."[3]

"With his shoulders He will overshadow thee and under His wings shalt thou trust."[4]

Who but God could have brought together figures so expressive of power and tenderness! How close we must be folded in His embrace for His shoulders to overshadow us! How widespread and vigilant must be those protecting wings to shelter us every one! Under such guardianship what shall we lack, whom shall we fear?

"Be not solicitous, therefore, saying: What shall we eat, or what shall we drink, or wherewith shall we be clothed? For your Father knoweth that you have need of all these things. Seek ye, therefore, first the kingdom of God and His justice and all these things shall be added unto you." Let us note, however, note carefully, the condition which ensures this specially loving care and protection. We must seek first the kingdom of God,

---

1 Life of Mary Ward   2 Deut 33:26   3 Ps. 36:5
4 Ps. 90:4

that is, His interests, His service. And then—nothing doubting—we may cast ourselves with our whole weight upon Him.

The very hairs of our head are numbered. We know this. Yet how many of us talk at times as if we believed in chance. St. Basil provides us with a remedy against what are called the mischances of life: "When things do not turn out as we wish, let us wish them to turn out as they do," which is only another way of acknowledging that all our ways are prepared.

On a journey we expect reasonable care will be taken to provide against accidents. When royalty travels, precautions are multiplied. But what are they all compared with the eternal foresight that has planned our road to heaven! On looking back we shall see something of it, but our assurance of this does not, apparently, authorize trust for the future. A failure, the death or estrangement of a friend, changes the prospect before us, and instead of seeing in this a necessary turn of the road, we give ourselves up for lost. Why? Because we see only a little way; God sees all the way home.

"A little child shall lead them."

Reggie was of a practical turn of mind. Applying himself one evening to his home lessons, a bright idea struck him. He would turn to account his newly-acquired knowledge of Bills of Parcels.

Next morning his mother found on her plate a small piece of paper, and was aware of being intently watched as she read the contents:

Mother, Dr. to Reggie	£ s. d.
For weding garden twice	.2
For picking guzberys	.1
For catching cattypillers	.3
For dusting mantelpeace in drawing room .	.2
For going messyges to auntie three times .	.3
For posting letters	.1
Total:	10

The bill was acknowledged with a smile and the promise that it should be settled next day. It was Mother's turn then to watch as Reggie in delight took the shilling from his plate and proceeded to read an accompanying paper:

Reggie, Dr. to Mother	£ s. d.
For nursing through a dangerous illness . . .	Nothing
For sitting up many nights with him	Nothing
For providing Birthday treats every year . .	Nothing
For taking to Zoo and buying buns for bears	Nothing
For warm clothes in the winter	Nothing
For good meals during eight years	Nothing
For mending his socks every week	Nothing
For taking to seaside every summer	Nothing
Total:	Nothing

As he read, his face showed a change of expression and a tear stole down his cheek. At last he slid off his chair, came over to his mother, stuffed the shilling into her hand, and with his arms round her neck whispered "Mummy!"

Trust in His Fatherhood

"A little child shall lead them."

"My Soul, what hast thou done for God?
Look o'er thy misspent years and see:
See first what thou hast done for God,
And then what God has done for thee."
— Faber.

VI

Trust in His Wisdom

"Thou hast made all things in wisdom."—Ps. 103:24

ONE OF the safest instincts of childhood and a valuable asset in early education is the child's faith in its father's wisdom as well as in his love. This accounts for the comparative ease with which its desires are relinquished, good habits are fostered, and harmful things are kept out of its way—supposing always that judicious training has begun before God-implanted instincts have been warped.

So long as we are in this world we are all children in our Father's nursery, and whilst outgrowing childishness, as St. Paul enjoins, we have to retain our childlike intuitions. The little child set to teach Apostles is but one instance of our Lord's insistence on this truth.

St. Paul says: "As long as the heir is a child…he is under tutors and governors until the time appointed by the father."[1] He may be heir to a cottage or to a throne, but his position of dependence and subjection remains the same. And we,

---
1 Galat. 4:1-2

too, are children, weak and ignorant, subjected to long and painful training as a preparation for our inheritance. Not much reflection is required to see ourselves as needy heirs, travelling in a foreign land for the sake of the valuable experience offered and the many reminders that we are not at home. Our tasks are marked out for us. As a rule we are not consulted, but find ourselves continually confronted by the tutors and governors appointed by the father. Who and what are they?

The persons and the events, all the various influences that bear upon our daily lives, those we welcome, those we would repel if we could. In all these causes and their combinations a lively faith sees the divine action, "the Spirit of God moving upon the waters," decreeing, permitting, guiding to a final purpose all that happens.

What concentration of thought, what summing up of resource, what readjustment of plans go to the perfecting of a work that a man considers to be his own creation. Should Infinite Power and Love condescend to make some work pre-eminently Its own, how wonderful will be the interest, how lavish the expenditure brought to bear upon it! From all eternity the design of a Mother of God was in the Mind of God. Would not all that He deemed necessary or suitable to such a transcendent dignity be provided?— No flaw in the material, nothing lacking in the glory of the design or in the execution. At an infinite cost the price will be paid, and the way of this chosen creature be prepared: "In the beginning and before all ages was I created." Because of a plenitude of grace, absolute freedom of will would be coupled with perfect fidelity to its least impulse.

How will the Wisdom of God have followed this, His own work, throughout its course; with what complacency have regarded it: when it returned in absolute perfection to His hands!

All this—the Incarnation being decreed—we accept as a corollary. The Christian instinct divined it. The Church has declared it. We admire and rejoice but are not surprised.

But that the Wisdom of God should have planned an inferior work, one that of set purpose would cross His design continually; that He should patiently and perpetually modify His ideal and make good the results of our wrong-doing—this is almost beyond belief, yet it is the happy experience of every one of us. And further:

Every child of Adam can say in his own measure and degree what the Church puts upon the lips of the Mother of God: "From the beginning and before all ages was I created." "To the Lord was His own work known from the beginning."[1] We are each and all so much His own work that to no other would He entrust the assignment of our place in His universal plan, with all the circumstances and details of our lives. The glory and the happiness He has in view for us is so far beyond anything we could conceive, that His Wisdom alone is equal to the task of preparing us for it. He, the Father, must appoint the tutors and governors who are to train us.

Naturally, such training must cost, always entail effort, often sacrifice and pain. Are we going to grudge it and to murmur? Does it not suffice the heirs to know that the appointments are the Father's choice?

---

1   Acts 15:18

The various theories which in these days of ours attack the Christian faith, have their little spell of notoriety. They pass away and give place to others. But their influence on immature and impressionable minds will remain. Are the children in our public schools to be exposed to such loosening of the hold of religion and of the moral law as threatens them? If the earlier chapters of *Genesis*, that speak of Creation, are dismissed today, the later, that treat of God's Commandments on Sinai, will be rejected tomorrow as out of sympathy with the age and inconsistent with the further advance of Science. Considering our boys and girls simply as subjects of the State, may they be taught doctrines subversive of social order, and their irresponsibility for crimes which the law visits with tremendous penalties?

Whilst anti-Christian teaching was finding voice in Westminster Abbey, a generous testimony to the Catholic Church was being given in the North by a Protestant Canon.[1] From the pulpit of York Minister came a warning note. "England," the preacher told his hearers, "is rapidly ceasing to be Christian. The lack of any clear religious teaching in most English schools is a cause of widespread demoralisation and a leading factor in making England no longer a Christian land in any true sense of the word...." He charged the Church of England with failure in its work for the preservation of religion among the English people, and pointed to the work being done in this respect by the Catholic Church. "We shall be roused," said the Canon, "from our lethargy and sleep to find the Church of Rome in

---
1 Canon E. Berry, Vicar of Drypool, Hull

this England of ours in an impregnable position...gripping tighter and tighter the education of our youth.... Except in a few limited spots, all the denominational religious teaching, even to our Protestant children, is being given by Roman Catholic teachers in Roman Catholic schools." The preacher bewailed the liberty that is becoming license—so much talk of encouraging in young people, even in children, what is known as "self-expression," so little of self-control and duty, such fear of "repression," that all sense of authority is disappearing.

Whilst deploring with the Canon these signs of the times, we may be grateful that our Cardinal Archbishop is able to bear out the above testimony to our schools by the assurance that "the work of education in accordance with the principles of the Catholic Faith is, happily, always extending its influence in this country...giving close attention to new problems as they arise, and reviewing the old problems in the light of more recent research."[1]

No wonder that our Bishops and Catholic laity are determined to strain every nerve to preserve our schools; that Cardinal Bourne declares this will be the principal issue at the General Election of 1929, and that His Eminence wishes it to be put clearly before the electorate all over the country. He points out that the non-provided schools—Catholic, Anglican, Non-conformist—are the only alternative to the State-built Council Schools; that, were the dual system swept away, and the non-provided schools to disappear, the poor would be deprived of their rights, and working-class parents of their liberty of choice

---
1 The Sower, Foreword by H. E. Cardinal Bourne, Sept. 1927

when seeking a school for their children—a liberty which poor parents enjoy equally with the well-to-do. This, said His Eminence, is the merest justice. There is no reason why those who hold that definite religious instruction is essential—an idea that is perfectly legitimate and deeply rooted in the history of the country—should be regarded as claiming a privilege for which they ought to pay. All must have a chance. The State can only come in to give free education so long as it does not infringe the rights of parents. To secure this right to all, demands new legislation in favour of non-provided schools. If not the whole, at least a large part of the cost of these schools ought to come out of the public purse.

The appeal of Cardinal Bourne for a national campaign in defense of our Catholic schools derives additional force from the happenings in Russia.

Viewing without alarm the destruction of Christianity with which Russia is threatened by the Cheka, certain parents in the autumn of 1927 sent over their children to come under the same influence.

To uproot in that mighty country of 150 million people, all religion, all belief in God, the Cheka had prohibited even in the home any worship of God and all religious teaching. For three hours every week all children between the ages of seven and twelve were bound to receive instruction from the "Communist Catechism," which overthrows all Christian belief. Teachers were compelled—many of them sorely against their will—to teach that there is no God, and that only when children reach the age of eighteen may they choose to which religious sect, if to any, they wish to belong. And because at home parents did their utmost to counteract the results of such atheistic teaching, they were forbidden under severe penalties to interfere in the education of their children—a matter declared to be for the State alone.

To prevent any parental influence, children were free to leave home and live in houses provided by the State called "*internats*," a kind of communal homes, where, completely independent of their parents, they were fed, clothed, and housed by the Government. In spite of all that mothers could do, boys and girls, under twelve, left home to go to these "internats." Any remonstrance of parents was denounced to the Cheka and punished.

These Russian children were all of them future Soviet propagandists to be employed in spreading communism in their villages and districts. Their position gives us some idea of the terrible condition of the young in Soviet Russia, and of the peril to our children if Communism should spread further afield. Yet a party of English children whose parents accepted an invitation from Moscow went over on a visit to see and fraternize with companions such as these!

As a contrast to the lot of these unfortunate children of Russia, we may quote a touching letter from Cardinal Hlond, Archbishop of Posen Gnesen, written to his mother immediately after being created a member of the Sacred College:

Dear Mother,
    The Holy Father has graciously made me a Cardinal of the Holy Roman Catholic Church. With deep gratitude

Trust in His Wisdom

I turn my heart and mind towards you, my dear Mother, and write my first letter to you.

When I consider the ways in which God's Providence leads me, your image is always before me. Better than many learned pedagogues you instilled into the souls of your children a strong foundation of life, based upon faith and the Divine Law. And, as you knew yourself how to pray sincerely and fervently, you taught us children earnest prayer, in which I find courage and confidence in God to this day.

You showed to us the way to happiness, teaching us not to be indolent, but to be strong in character, and to work, and you taught us to love duty and to desire to carry out our duties sincerely and gladly.

Therefore, nowhere but in the nobility and the sublimity of your simple and devoted heart is to be found the beginning of that way on which God's grace guided me and led me to that which generally is called dignity, but which after the conception of our family, means a higher fulfillment in work and devotion.

On this day, on which the grace of the Holy Father is shining with its splendour over our Upper Silesian hut, I thank you heartily that you were a good mother to me, and ask for your pious prayer that I may by my work serve the honour of God, the cause of His Holy Church, and the happiness of my father....

With gratitude and piety, I kiss your hands, hard from work, and ask your motherly benediction on the way that duty will lead me.

Your son August, Cardinal.

VII

Trust in His Will

"Yea, Father, for so hath it seemed good in Thy sight"—Matt. 11:26

THE CHILD'S instinctive sense of its own ignorance and weakness makes it turn to its father in all needs and troubles. Its response to his care—a response to which in early years it is so easily guided—is gratitude, obedience and trust.

And these are the dispositions our Heavenly Father looks for in His children. Our Elder Brother, who came to reveal to us the Father and the Father's Will, has so emphasized this by word and example, that in twenty-eight places the Gospels mention it.

Our Father would have us content with His disposal of us, with the joys and the sorrows He sends, the uncertainties in which we are left, with pain of body and trouble of mind; in everything we ought to abandon ourselves to Him to be content with God.

To throw the past, the present, and the future into the infinite abyss of God's mercy and indulgence, this is to find joy in our faith, to live in security and peace: "My Father, let me see as You see, judge of things as You judge, do as You want me to do, and be what You desire."

Joy of spirit is truly the life of faith. But the road is uphill. To follow it we must resolve to accept and rejoice in all that God sends or permits. This is to rejoice "*in the Lord*" as the Apostle bids us. In Heaven we shall find our absolute content in the good pleasure of God. But we need not wait till then, for St. Paul says: "Rejoice always," therefore it cannot be an impossibility. Happiness does not depend on the satisfaction of our desires. Or rather, it is just this on which it does depend if our desire is always the accomplishment of God's desires, put in a safe place, high above the so-called mischances of this world which can so easily reach and wreck it. To see the Will of God brought to us by all persons and events and to make it welcome at once, this is to rejoice always. This is to be conformed to the mind of our dear Lord and Master, to say with Him: "Ita, Pater: Yea, Father, for so hath it seemed good in Thy sight." "Never mind my sight, *my* narrow, selfish views. What I really want is to range my will alongside of Yours always, always. And as soon as I see it. Let there be no interval between Your Will and my loving adhesion to it. Let me always will or not will the same with You.

Asked if she had a devotion to the Will of God, a child replied: "I don't know that I have; I prefer His good pleasure." It is a loving distinction and made an immediate convert of the questioner. St. Thérèse of Lisieux would probably have owned to the same preference: "Before asking anything for myself or others," she says, "I used to look into the Face of God to see if I could read there any unwillingness to give what I asked. I would not give Him the pain of having to refuse me." "Grant me always to will and desire that which is most acceptable to Thee, and which pleaseth Thee best," says à Kempis. Could we but come to this! To wish to be precisely and solely what God desires is our only reasonable disposition as His creatures. But it means self-renunciation. It involves nothing less than an entire surrender of ourselves and our interests into His Hands. And this is not a disposition that comes all at once. It can only be the result of Love. But His grace is ready to help us. As a Father He is keenly interested in each one of us; is so anxious that His plan for our happiness should mature, that He is only too ready to help when we want to co-operate with Him by falling in with His designs.

Try Him when a scheme upon which you have set your heart breaks down. He has allowed it. Why, you will know some day. Meantime do not let this best of fathers have the disappointment of seeing a cloud on the face of His child, another project for your good turning out a failure. Look up instead, and smile: "Dear Father, this is hard, certainly, but I am not going to spoil by churlishness anything You think good to send. After all, I only want what You want, as You know." Take the joy this will be to Him, in place of the satisfaction you looked for. That would soon have passed. The other will never pass, but will be shared with Him for ever.

Habit will make this easier as time goes on, till at last the act of contented, nay, cheerful acceptance of all that God does, will come almost spontaneously: "It will be a hard winter, blessed be God!" How often one may hear a sentence like this from Irish lips!

Trust in His Will

Into most lives there comes a crisis. How much depends on it, God only knows. Happy those whom it finds going through life like a child with its hand in its father's, taking joys and sorrows as they come. The crisis will find them ready. It may be an accident—a death, perhaps—and the whole aspect of your future is changed. You are staggered. But the Hand to which you have clung in the past holds you fast. Your first impulse may be to turn on the cause you think accountable. Look further. God is behind it, waiting for that turning of your will to His which will bring Him to your help, that *giving in to Him* to which He is urging you. The effort may seem impossible. There may be a rising of rebellion or of despair. But He is there. Instead of relaxing your hold on His Hand, keep it fast. It may be the driest, most painful act of resignation, but His pitying Heart will be content. What He asks is not feeling. Else, how would our Lord have prayed in the Garden as He did? He will say of you as He said of Magdalen: "She hath done what she could." That hard act of giving in to God held in it all the essence of conformity:

"Yea, Father, for so hath it seemed good in Thy sight."

"Fear not for I am with thee!"

In that mutual pressure of the hand is strength—and peace.

Nurse offers its medicine to the sick child—and it turns wearily away. The father comes in, takes the cup and with a smile puts it to the reluctant lips. The draught is taken to the last drop, eyes all the time on the father's face… "A little child shall lead them!"

All this, it may be said, supposes great grace and an exceptional state.

Father de Ravignan replies: "A great grace, certainly; an exceptional state, No." With the divine assistance it is within the reach of us all. The Beatific Vision in the Soul of our Lord during His Agony shows us that even in the keenest suffering of body and mind, of weariness and disgust, the soul in its highest part may remain contented with God, and, like St. Paul, superabound with joy in the midst of tribulation. Why wait for Heaven when our Lord bids us say daily and for the happenings of each day: "Thy Will be done on earth as it is done in Heaven?"

In truth we are hard to please. With all our self-sufficiency there is in our heart of hearts the creature's instinctive trust in the Creator, the child in its Father; in His Will rather than in its own. Ignorant of the trials that circumstances may bring about, which of us would dare to choose our own life—that is, the life of an adventurer for seventy or eighty years? On the other hand, who would desire to die this coming year and forego all the blessings a further term of life and meriting may bring? Our only safety is to leave the future to God, and take in childlike trust what He sends. This we feel. And yet—when His appointments do not meet with our approval we grumble as if we could have chosen better for ourselves—we who dare not choose at all! Truly the heart of man is inscrutable, and the Divine Patience—Infinite!

Thy Will, then, my God, be done on earth as it is done in Heaven! This is my will and desire. For this I make over to Thee my liberty and all *my will*. I would rather have the lowest place in Thy Kingdom by Thy Will than a higher by my own. But I will not willingly have anything lower than the one Thou hast appointed for me, the one to which tend all the graces Thou hast given me, the one where I may give Thee throughout eternity the greatest glory. O that I might be known not by such or such gifts, as by the simple name of "*My pleasure in her.*"[1]

---

[1] Isaias 62:4

VIII

Trust in His Mercy

"For if we sin we are thine"—Wis. 11:2

THERE are spiritual writers who represent Almighty God in the Old Law as terrible, exacting, swift to punish. This is hardly what His own inspired Word tells us of Himself. He is always entreating His faithless people to return to Him and be forgiven: "Is it My will that a sinner should die, saith the Lord God, and not that he should be converted and live?" "Be converted and do penance, and iniquity shall not be your ruin." "Make to yourselves a new heart. Why will you die, O House of Israel!" "Cease to do perversely. Learn to do well.... And then come and accuse Me, saith the Lord; if your sins be as scarlet they shall be made white as snow."

And how do those speak of Him who even amid the shadows of that olden time knew Him and found Him "sweet"?

"Behold God is my Saviour, I will deal confidently and will not fear," says Isaias. "Thou our God, art gracious and true, patient, and ordering all things in mercy." "For if we sin we are Thine."

"Afterwards He was seen upon earth and conversed with men."[1] The approach was infinitely nearer and tenderer than anything man had been led to expect. The Incarnation and its extension in the Eucharist is a union of God with us so astounding that the possibility of it could never have entered the mind of man. Its revelation to us of the character of our Heavenly Father and His Divine Son and of the Holy Spirit who has been called "What is sweetest in God," will be a Mystery of unfathomable love and joy to us throughout eternity.

And to think that more than half of the human race know nothing of all this! Of the generosity with which God gave His Son to the world that the world might be saved by Him. Of the depths of the Divine Mercy and Compassion as disclosed in the parables and in every detail of our Lord's life on earth! To think that the Gospels can be to so many of us who call ourselves His followers—all but unknown records!

The first thing foretold of Him before His coming was that He should be called Jesus, for He should save His people from their sins. This was to be the very purpose for which He came. He said of Himself: "I am come to seek and to save that which was lost." His first appearance in public was amongst sinners, coming to His Precursor to be baptised in their company. He sought their society and was known to seek it so that He came to be called "the Friend of publicans and sinners." He made them welcome always and in His parables compared them favourably with others. It was not the merciless pressure of the crowd upon Him from morning till night, not persistence in a petition

---

1 Bar. 3:38

even to importunity, that met with remonstrance, nor an evil life that He rebuked with severity. What wounded Him, what He rebuked in His disciples was want of faith. What He praised and rewarded in those who came to Him in trouble was almost always—faith. Why? Because if it is not the highest of all virtues it is the root of all. Faith and trust so mingle as to be almost indistinguishable, and trust, as we see from the Gospels, could win anything and everything from Christ our Lord. To be trusted with their sorrows was a confidence He valued in the troubled. To be trusted with their sins, above all.

In His parables there was the gentleness of Him who loved to call Himself the Son of man; who drew from the homely things of daily life what would appeal to the poor and lowly—the woman seeking anxiously for her lost groat; the shepherd whose flock has been left in the desert for the sake of the one sheep lost in the mountains; the prodigal for whose homecoming there must be the father's kiss, the first robe and ring, welcoming music and a feast.

The fact that all this is our Lord's conception, every detail the expression of His own mind and heart, is what captivates us. In this lies the charm of His parables, that they give us the Truth, that they translate for us the Most Holy Trinity, the Divine Family into which we are admitted, with whom we are to spend our eternity.

It was all so new yet so familiar to the downtrodden and the suffering, the innocent and the sinful, that they thronged Him and flocked after Him into the desert—men, women and children, content to be day after day without shelter, rest, or food, so they might be with Him, look upon His Face, hear the tones of His voice, drink in teaching that reached the soul of each, and without bruise or sting healed its hidden sores. It was because He spake as no man ever spake that they fled from their scribes and Pharisees to the feet of Jesus of Nazareth. They knew He could read their souls, yet they were not afraid of Him. They could take Him to their homes, and to the bedside of their sick. Children might play about Him or climb on His knee. Mothers told how He would not have their noisy little ones driven from Him but took them into His arms and embraced and blessed them. Publicans found that He did not refuse their hospitality nor disdain the roof of a Gentile centurion. Nay, more. A sinner had dared to intrude where He sat at meat in the house of a Pharisee and unrebuked had washed His feet with her tears. One, taken before Him for judgment, that meant a fearful death, had heard only: "Hath no man condemned thee? Neither will I condemn thee. Go, and now sin no more."

It was joy to these simple friends of His that the scribes and Pharisees never caught Him in His speech: "Which of you," He had said, "shall convince Me of sin?" The lawyers heckled Him in vain, and quite easily were sent away discomfited. Interrupted in His discourse, he was never ruffled, wearied was never fretful, stern at times was never harsh. When evening came and the last disputant or suppliant had left Him, He would steal away and on a mountain side give Himself to prayer. Unless, indeed, a timorous soul, ashamed or afraid to come to Him by day sought Him at night, for such a one He was ready at all hours.

What most of all surprised His hearers was His extraordinary readiness to forgive sin. Coming upon the paralytic who for eight-and-thirty years had lain at the Probatica Pond, vainly asking help "of the multitude standing in the place," Jesus of Nazareth had not only healed him, but finding him later in the Temple had said: "Sin no more lest some worse thing happen to thee." Neither for body nor for soul had there been petition, but His eyes filled with tears quickly, nor was He ever known to look upon suffering unmoved.

Teaching once in a crowded room before "Pharisees and doctors of the law that were come out of every town of Galilee and Jerusalem," He was interrupted by a man being let down through the roof on a mat and laid on the ground before Him for cure.... There was no displeasure at the disturbance. On the contrary the young Teacher seemed to be awaiting the sufferer. Gently steadying the bed as it came down, He reassured the intruder. "Be of good heart, son, thy sins are forgiven thee."

"He blasphemeth," thought some of the scribes, "Who can forgive sins but God only?"

"Seeing their thoughts, Jesus said: 'Which is it easier to say, Thy sins are forgiven thee, or to say, Arise, take up thy bed and walk? But that you may know that the Son of Man hath power on earth to forgive sins,' He saith to the man: 'Arise, take up thy bed and go into thy house.' And he arose and taking up his bed went his way in the sight of all, so that all wondered and glorified God that gave such power to men."

It was the only instance of our Lord working a miracle to prove a doctrine. There was no petition either for the cure of the body or of the soul. But His power as man to forgive sin had been questioned. And to prove that power before "Pharisees and doctors of the law come out of every town of Galilee and Judea," the miracle was wrought, "that you may know that the Son of Man hath power on earth to forgive sins...." Whether the wise and prudent yielded to the evidence of their senses, we are not told, but it is distinctly stated that "the multitude seeing it wondered and glorified God that gave such power to men."

The first thing foretold of the Messias at His coming was that His name should be called Jesus, for He should save His people from their sins. But the institution of the Sacrament of Mercy whereby His own power as Son of Man to forgive sin was passed on to His Church, this He reserved for the glad Day of His Resurrection.

Gathered together in the Upper Room on the evening of the first day of the week, the disciples were talking of the various apparitions of Christ, confirmed by St. Peter, when, suddenly, Jesus "stood in the midst and said to them: Peace be to you. When He had said this He breathed on them and said to them: As the Father hath sent Me I also send you. Receive ye the Holy Ghost. Whose sins you shall forgive they are forgiven them and whose you shall retain they are retained."

Strange words, they seem, for that first greeting! To have found excuse for their abandonment of Him in His hour of need, to have comforted them in their confusion and their fears by the assurance that they had forfeited neither His favour nor His love—this would have been like Him. But no. His Heart was too glad and too generous for any allusion to the past. It was so full of the world's deepest need, the forgiveness of sin, that He went straight to this fruit of His Passion and brought it with Him as His first gift to us on the very Day of His Resurrection, as the source of all joy and hope to the end of time and throughout eternity.

He said therefore to them again, "Peace be to you!" A two-fold peace—for themselves, bringing not assurance of forgiveness only but reinstatement in their vocation. And through them peace to men, as angels had sung at Bethlehem.

Can we wonder, then, at that first joyful greeting and announcement on Easter Day? And that the Church makes it her utmost endeavour to bring all men within reach of that Sacrament of Peace, that saving "penance and remission of sins," which by His last words on Ascension Day our Divine Master ordered to be preached in His Name to all nations, beginning at Jerusalem.

"*Plentiful Forgiveness.*" One cause why God is Incomprehensible to us is that He is at once like and so unlike ourselves. From the fact that we are made in His image and likeness, that He would have us think of Him as our Father, and of ourselves as "most dear children," we come to form a picture of Him, faint, indeed, and imperfect, but true so far as it goes. We bring together all that is noblest, tenderest, most attractive in human fatherhood, magnify it as far as possible, and then believe we have some idea of the love and solicitude of our Father who is in heaven.

But when there is question of the forgiveness we need so often, anything like parallel fails. What earthly father would pardon as He pardons, over and over again, and with the same readiness, fullness and trust each time as if it were the first? It is the backsliding we find it so hard to overlook in one another. Repetition is such aggravation of offence that we think it a valid reason for mistrusting sincerity. If forgiveness is not withheld altogether it is given grudgingly.

How different is God from us here! He knows how unworthy we are of His pardon. He sees that before night we shall be coming to Him for it afresh. The selfishness of our contrition, the weakness of our good purposes, the callousness with which we shall resist grace, the rashness with which we shall run into temptation and neglect prayer—all this He knows. Yet, as if there were weakness only, and no negligence nor malice in our falls, as if the hurt to ourselves, not the injury to Him, were all that had to be considered, as if our own pain and disappointment at our repeated failings called for nothing but the soothing we give to the stumbling child, He runs to meet us, raises us, and folds us in His arms. He promises to forgive and forget, to make good our losses, and supply us with more abundant help for another time. No reproach, no reminder of broken resolutions, no distrust, no diminution—provided we have not forfeited it altogether by mortal sin—of that treasure of sanctifying grace which is to be the measure of our eternal reward. Even when we completely turn our back upon Him by grievous sin, and for some miserable gratification, part with His friendship, and with all the merit His grace had helped us to acquire, the moment we recover sanctifying grace by a good confession or an act of perfect contrition, this treasure in its entirety is restored to us. Unlike the bankrupts of this world, we have not to begin all over again, but our original store is given back to us as if nothing had been forfeited.

Truly, "*plentiful forgiveness*"! And not only to be had for the asking, and for any sin, however grievous, and after any number of lapses, but pressed upon us, as if to accept it and fling ourselves once more into the arms of our heavenly Father were a boon we were conferring upon Him. It is all so unlike our dealings with one another that we find its reality hard to bring home to ourselves.

When Peter, thinking to show himself generous to his brother in the matter of forgiveness—no doubt there was friction at times, and, after all, the boat was his—asked if seven times would do, our Lord hastened to give His first Vicar a much needed lesson as to the application of the new Sacrament to be confided to him.

"Seven times! Nay, seventy times seven!"

Supposing seven times had been assigned as the limit, seven in our lives, how we should have trembled as we neared the term. How excusable should we have found the intervals between our confessions! But no. "Come as often as you need forgiveness," says our Lord. "Many of My servants come daily"—a sad waste of grace, we might consider! We hang back when He calls us to Him. We mistrust the magnificence of His generosity. We think to honour Him by refusing to sit down at His Banquet because of the daily dust that clings to us.

What if we were to deal with Him after a more childlike fashion! Not, certainly, to bewail less our sins and shortcomings, but to accept more simply and more gratefully His free forgiveness of them, to return to Him more promptly and more trustfully after each fall, thinking more of the disappointment *to Him* than of punishment for ourselves? Would not this give Him greater glory than the bitterness of self-reproach or the despondency of wounded self-love?

"Would you mind forgiving me once more, Mummy?"
"And why should I mind, darling?"
"Well, you see, because it's so soon again."

Our Father's love is so tender that He would never have us oppressed by the sense of distance from Him. In the very moment we are conscious of sin, His arms are outstretched to us. Let us yield ourselves to them and be drawn into their shelter. The swift return to Him after every fall costs something to our mistrustful hearts. But the humility it involves, and the peace it brings, as well as the teaching and practice of all the saints prove that it is the most acceptable reparation we can make Him, the quickest means of overcoming our faults, and a sure way to the knowledge and love of our Father in Heaven. "If you feel afraid of God," says St. Augustine, "throw yourself into His arms: He will not draw back to let you fall."

A fire broke out at night in a four-storied house and spread rapidly. Mother and children were got out, and then the father could only watch with the crowd the work of destruction and the clouds of smoke that poured down into the street.

Suddenly from a high window came a piercing cry. A little figure stood outside on the sill.

"Jump, Stan!" shouted the father. "I am here and will catch you. Jump!"

"I can't see you, Dad. It's all smoke."

"I see *you* and I'll catch you. Don't be afraid. Jump! Quick!"

The child jumped and fell…into the father's arms.

"Father, into Thy Hands I commend my spirit."

"In the hour of my death call me and bid me come to Thee."

"In Thee, O Lord, have I hoped I shall not be confounded."

IX

Trust in His Love

"O taste and see that the Lord is sweet."—Ps. 33:99

LOVE in human beings is measured by its subject; its object; its extravagances; its craving for a return of love from the object loved. Some persons have undoubtedly a larger capacity for love than others; there are those in whom it can amount to heroism.

One love kills another. The child begins by loving and grasping its sweets and its toys. As years go by, it outgrows these inclinations and transfers its love to those about it, to those who are good to it, to animals. Then intellectual objects—music, art, books—engage its affections. Friends desire each other's company, the home circle, the poor; religious life, perhaps, or marriage absorb attention.

Love shows itself also by its extravagances. All history testifies to this truth. We have only to see what is going on around us every day; the materials for *Punch* and for the greater part of the jokes that are passed about amongst us are furnished thus.

We long, moreover, to possess what we love and to give to it. No matter how costly, how trifling, how useless a thing may be, it will serve our turn so long as it is something to give.

And love desires a return of love, even in the case of an animal; a man trains and fondles a dog, and is content if only it hangs about him and shows a return of affection.

The love of the saints for God is revealed by all these characteristics:

The love of all reaches the heroic. There can be no question of limitation. The Object is simply Infinite: "the measure of love is to be without measure." Their care to avoid all that could displease or be disagreeable to Him; their desire to think His thoughts, to fall in with His ways, to love what He loves, to hate what He hates, to see Him loved by all; counting no cost in His service, sharing with Him suffering as well as joy,—this is love, "not in word and in tongue, but in deed and in truth." The saints look at the Crib and the Cross and the Altar, and their cry is: "*Quid retribuam?* What shall I render to Him?"

And the love of God for us—Is it shown in our ways?

St. Luke says that on Thabor Moses and Elias spoke to our Lord of "the excess" which He should accomplish in Jerusalem. But was not His love excess from first to last? The most marvellous thing about it is the disproportion between the Subject and the object. What should we think of the man who so loved his dog as to wish to become a dog in order to be on its level? God has taken our nature, and in the Incarnation, the Redemption, the Eucharist, Communion every morning, if we will, gives us Himself with a prodigality that looks like foolishness. The only thing that can in any way account for this seeming recklessness of love is the fact that, like us, He loves His handiwork; we are the work of His hands.

And, then, God is our Father. As if Creator were tie not close nor tender enough, He would adopt us as His children, designing for us as our inheritance His own beatitude. He loves us to the extent of bringing us into the society of the Ever-Blessed Trinity, giving us His only Son to be our Brother, our Teacher, our Mediator, our life, our very food. How has He not with Him given us all things?

The love of God for us is an individual love. Because He made us, He knows us through and through and loves in each one of us that which makes us what we are—ourselves and not another, a special creation—what, when perfected, will give us our individual claim to His love throughout eternity. In spite of our defects and our limitations He loves each one of us with more than the indulgence of our most intimate friend. According to a boy's definition, "a friend is someone who knows all about you and likes you all the same"—true as far as it goes, but sadly short of the mark.

Why do we think our Heavenly Father hard and difficult to please? When He gets us safely into Heaven He will say to us: "I have carried thee as a man is wont to carry his little son all the way that you have come to this place." All our ways are prepared. He would trust to no other, however wise or kind, the preparation of those ways. Every step is foreseen and planned by Himself.

"But they are hard ways," we say.

For a little while. We shall not think so presently. And meantime why cannot we trust Him when we can glorify Him by our trust? We do not expect our children to think hardly of us because of the necessary discipline through which they must pass to fit them for their inheritance. There may be much blundering on our part, much needless suffering on theirs, yet we expect them to trust us. Shall we mistrust Him who has provided down to the smallest details of our lives, making all things—even the most untoward and painful—work together for our final happiness?

As a little child St. Thérèse of Lisieux liked to walk home at night, eyes shut, her hand in her father's, guided by him even through difficult ways. And so she went joyfully on her road through life, her hand in her Heavenly Father's. They were hard ways at times through which He led her, but her joyful trust never failed. And now it looks as if He could refuse her nothing. If only we could trust Him like the saints! It is the greatest mistake to look upon prosperity here as a sure sign of His favour. Money, health, success are not His best gifts, and He rarely gives them to His dearest friends. Are we so sure they would be good *for us?* He is patient with us almost beyond belief, but we tie His hands by our mistrust.

Like us, God looks for a return of love.

He has no need of my goods, but He has made over to His needy children His right to my love and service.

Yes, *service.* I am not in this world for my own satisfaction, to have a good time, nor even to save my own soul—solely. "This is My Commandment, that you love one another," says our Lord, and that, "not in word nor in tongue but in deed and in truth."

"And how is that?"

"As I have loved you."

Long and deeply have His servants pondered and acted upon that word "as." They have spent themselves and are spending themselves daily in the service of His "least brethren," knowing this is in very deed to serve Christ Himself. They take Him at His word when He said: "Whatsoever you do to one of My least you do it to Me"—a kind word, a cup of cold water, a trifling alms—"Whatsoever"—a harsh reply, an unkind insinuation—"Whatsoever."

"As I have loved you." The word "as" is relative and determined by circumstances. At Nazareth the Child helped His Mother as His baby hands and strength enabled Him. In the Temple at twelve years old He was found among the doctors *as* His Father's service required. Later on came the laborious days of the Public Life. "As I have loved you" in the Passion meant the death of the Cross.

So with His servants. They cannot all serve lepers or go out to China to rescue babies. We must take God's service as He lays it at our door or puts it within our reach. Only let it be worthy of its noble name and adapted to our circumstances and capabilities. The staple of our life should be labour of mind or body; pleasure and excitement its refreshment, not its business. And let us remember that Home is the first apostolate. It is sad to note how every force that can loosen its hold and wreck its happiness is being directed against it. Reverent affection and submission to parents is now to a great extent banished even from the nursery, and in its stead has come to be tolerated an off-hand behaviour towards them in word and manner, a tendency to regard them rather as providers of pleasure than as those to whom at every stage of life we have duties of gratitude and reverent love.

Anything we can do to protect and brighten the home—our own first, and any other we can influence, is well worth an output of labour, ingenuity, and tact—by which we mean those little thoughtful attentions which do so much to strengthen its hold and make the wheels run smoothly. To keep this steadily before us is a worthier object than a constant round of excitement and pleasure. To lead a consistent Catholic life in our home and neighbourhood, utilising our opportunities and being ready for little sacrifices, is no small service of God. The holy Curé of Ars had no great natural talents. When his wonderful works were mentioned before him he smiled and said: "I only know one thing—I have never been afraid of trouble." Any one of whom the home can say *that*, is no ordinary servant of God.

To lead a Catholic life worthily is to teach at least by example, and spread the truth. But many of us feel the necessity of doing more than is of strict obligation, and in view of the pressing need, our Bishops urge such as are able to deepen their religious knowledge that they may be able to defend and explain our Faith to the ever-increasing numbers who seek information. Nay, they go so far as to say that Catholics who, neither by hearing nor reading seek to strengthen their faith, and go out into the world of today with no more preparedness to meet its questionings than the elementary teaching of the catechism they learned in their childhood, are in great danger of losing their faith altogether.

The number of priests in England, sadly insufficient at present, will be quite inadequate to the needs of the future; the laity must come forward. To be kind to a lonely convert, or, better still, a lapsed Catholic, to befriend a boy or girl leaving school for work, to take a non-Catholic to Benediction, or tactfully approach a stranger in the porch who would evidently welcome information—all helps. Goodwill readily sees its opportunity, and with the fields white unto harvest, why should the labourers be few?

The question: "*Quid retribuam?*" has been the beginning of many a fruitful life in the service of God. Not a few boys and girls at the end of their school course have an apostolate in view and devote a considerable portion of time to the study and labour it requires. Nor is this a passing phase; they have counted the cost. "Pray for me," writes one of these, "that I may stick to it. Novelty keeps one up at first. When that wears off and monotony begins to tell, it is then that things cost." He was under no delusion. To last, work must be done *for God*, not taken up as a fresh excitement to be dropped on the first pretext.

The departments of useful work now open to women widen continually. But let us see that external activities do not interfere with obligations at home. It is said that married women are being swept into endless committees to the prejudice of their children and home duties. This is to defeat the end in view. The public service has its claims. Yet, surely, the children come first. Their training and happiness must be the mother's first care. Should they doubt this—her influence over them is gone.

Is English home life, once so loved and guarded, in danger, then, of losing its hold? Those whose outlook is neither narrow nor pessimistic warn us that its foundations, assailed on every side, must give way at last, like the banks of an overcharged river, unless a remedy is found.

Let none of us say that our individual influence and action is too insignificant to be of any avail. True; "Unless the Lord guard the city the sentinel doth watch in vain." His grace and succour must save our country in its present need. But to all who have eyes to see, it must be plain that God *is* working for England at the present hour, working through the ministry of His Church. The blood of her martyrs is bearing fruit, and she calls on her children one and all to take part with her in garnering the harvest; to unite so closely with her and her Divine Head that His influence and action may flow through them to all around. "Freely," she says, "you have received, freely give."

"*Quid retribuam*," What shall *I* render, she puts on the lips of us all whenever we come to Mass. I cannot shift my responsibility on to another. It is a personal question and calls for a personal reply. My answer will mark the return of love for which my God looks from me.

X

Trust in His Tests

(I) "Tutors and Governors"

"Thou didst admonish and try them as a father."—Wis. 11:11

THE LOVE of God, like ours, has many modes of expression, or rather, our love, in so far as it is true, is but a faint shadow of His, with its invitations, its gifts, its sacrifices, its surprises and disguises, its joys and hopes and fears, and above all—*its tests*. What the stories of our nursery days told us of the course of true love, our human nature accepts as reliable and universal; indeed, as bearing upon it the marks of an origin above the experiences of this world and of human life. The dear old tales appeal to the true instincts of childhood to-day as centuries ago when they show us the good people suffering for a time but at length reaching the goal of all their desires, and the wicked prospering till the day of retribution comes; wrong being set right, the weak being helped against the strong, and invariably—the happy ending. So much is this a matter of course, that among all the marks which love in fairyland exacts and exhibits is that of—its tests.

How thoroughly the unspoilt mind approves the working out of this law! Why is our judgment less trustworthy in later life? Or why do we claim for ourselves exemption from the lot of the elect from Abel the just to the servants of God today?

An heir leaves a home where he has wanted for nothing. From his tastes being consulted constantly he has come to consider himself, if not everybody, at least somebody to be reckoned with. He goes to college, and lo! after the first hour of attentions finds himself… in the Common of Martyrs. "The best thing possible for him," say his friends, "and the sooner he makes the experiment, the better." And the sooner we all make the same discovery, the better for us—the realization that this world is meant to be school, not home, a place of training and trial, for it is exile no less than school.

This being so, it behooves us, not merely to accept the inevitable, but to turn to the best advantage our time of tutelage, with the subjection and the suffering it involves.

St. Paul tells us we are under tutors and governors… serving under the elements of the world;[1] as if trial and pain were so inseparable from our condition here on earth as to be the very elements of the world. And this after the curse has been taken away by the coming of Christ, who has changed the name of "punishment" to "trial," transferring it through grace from the inevitable to the meritorious.

Who and what are the tutors provided for us?

---

[1] Galat. 4:1, 3

As understood by St. Paul, they comprise all created things, animate and inanimate—persons, events, time, talents, joys, troubles, success, failure, health, sickness, life and death, all the influences brought to bear upon us in our passage through this world. In themselves these things are indifferent as to value for eternity. But in God's selection of them for us individually they are of inestimable worth, for on our use or misuse of them depends our eternal salvation. Each has a clearly defined task to accomplish, its limits assigned, its grace provided, its reward prepared.

To secure the end proposed, three things are necessary: We must recognize ourselves as being here by the appointment of our Father *for training*; we must trust His provision for us; and realize that for the longest life the school course is short; there is no margin for dawdling or waste.

A father gives much time and reflection to the selection of a tutor for his son. But the happiest choice does not of itself ensure success. Opportunity is not all. What would have started many a waif on a glorious career has been wasted on a prince. There must be cooperation if grace is to have its way with us. And this is specially true of the discipline of pain.

God cannot, or at any rate does not, work without the Cross. Could we look into the lives of the elect, toiling on the up-hill road today, we should see each one carrying his cross—not dragging, but *carrying* it, bearing it willingly, as a pledge of future glory, the price of a kingdom. For a little while it is the dark side that he sees, and then—the reverse for eternity.

As to many of the things God places at my disposal, I have to use my free-will, to carve out my future with the help of His grace. He will have me receive the kingdom prepared for me, not as an heir to whom it falls by right, but with the immensely added joy of a recompense earned. Hence I have to utilize my Christian common-sense as to use or abstinence, avoiding what would hinder the work I have in hand, using what helps, in the measure in which it helps. With regard to painful things, I have often no choice—my moods, duties, companions, the weather, petty annoyances of various kinds providing that element of pain which is not only the inevitable consequence of living in this world, but is the special provision of God for bringing me to rest and reward when this short life is done.

It is their faith that enables the servants of God to see—not chance nor ill-luck in what are called the mischances of life—but God's controlling Hand. This is the secret of their abiding peace. They have trained themselves to discern in all things the marvellous workings of Divine Providence for their good. Habit has made this supernaturally second nature, so that what at first cost effort and struggle has come through grace to be done gracefully and with abundant merit for eternity.

This Christian common sense makes His servants realize that having sent them here for the one purpose of working out their salvation by using aright the instruments He puts into their hands, God must have designed these as means to the end He had in view. He has given me the same common sense to view them from the same standpoint and to fall in loyally with His designs. Do I use it?

The servants of God on earth today are being raised to God by the same joys and sorrows that come *to us*, by the death of those they love, by sharp pains of body and soul, by the monotony of life. If we want to join them some day, must we not tread in their footsteps?

We wish we had their strong trust and their fortitude. We may have it by the strength that comes through prayer, by the sight of our Leader going before us, by the sound of His cheering voice, the grasp of His helping hand. Where He found comfort, we, too, shall find it, the comfort that means strength: "An Angel appeared," *confortans eum*, that is, strengthening Him.

Oh! those blessed words of the great Apostle, "tutors and governors *appointed by the Father.*" It was in that knowledge that our Elder Brother, the Heir by excellence, found support in "the excess," through which He had to pass, "the chalice which My Father hath given Me, shall I not drink it?" Can we not, like Him, trust the Father's appointment? Could any choice of ours be better? Is He not watching to see that trial shall never go too far? "Having joy set before Him, Christ endured the cross." Can we not endure a little while *with Him?*

It is helpful to look upon the trials sent by God as His *testing* of His servants. In these days freewill is practically denied by many, or considered, with life itself, as a grievance, involving issues as to which they were not consulted. Yet how eagerly opportunities with all their risks are being seized; the daily papers show the growing rage for record-making; airmen and air-women, swimmers, prizefighters, golfers, experts in any exciting pursuit to which tests can be applied, rouse worldwide enthusiasm, draw spectators in thousands, and create colossal fortunes. The fascination of tests is irresistible. With one exception. God offers His tests with their prizes, and not only do they arouse no interest, but too often they provoke resentment and rejection. How few, comparatively, think them worth an effort! In time of trouble our friends remind us that "Man's extremity is God's opportunity." Why not remember also that the tests of God are always man's opportunity, involving with His helpful grace, which is never wanting, not only no risk, but a glorious reward; "for *when he hath been proved* he shall receive the crown of life which God hath promised to them that love Him" (St. James 1:12)?

X
Trust in His Tests

(II) His Invitations

AMONG the forces that control our spiritual training, "tutors" may represent such as stimulate and encourage, "governors," those that act by way of authority.

To the first will belong the inspirations of the Holy Spirit which "prevent" us at every turn. Somewhere or other in its history our English word "prevent" seems to have taken a twist and swung round to a meaning the exact contrary of the original signification to which the etymology points. The technical and theological sense the Church retains in her Collect for the bestowal of that *prevenient* grace which originates all good thoughts and actions in order to salvation. "Prevent our actions by Thy holy inspirations,"—that is, start them as their prime mover, for without Thee we can do nothing. In the beginning the Spirit moved upon the waters, and from Him must come every impulse that wafts us on our way to Heaven.

When human pride rejected this doctrine, St. Augustine, the "Doctor of Grace," and St. Jerome came forward in its defense, and against the Pelagians and Semi-Pelagians it was defined that we are unable without God's help even to desire what will avail towards eternal life. With what thankfulness, then, must all who have reached salvation look back upon the countless actions which began, advanced, and happily ended by grace, have been crowned in Heaven with glory!

(1)

Look at the history of a divine inspiration. It has been a thought of God from eternity, a companion in the Divine Mind with the design of the Incarnation which is its final cause and purchase-price.

As long as God has been God that inspiration has been cherished by the Ever-Blessed Trinity—its way prepared from the beginning and advanced with the ages. Its hour come, it leaves the Bosom of God for an uncongenial sphere. Saints and angels see something of its potentialities and wish it God-speed, praying that the Will of God may be done on earth as it is in Heaven.

Its goal is a human heart—and there it knocks. With what result? Too often with Bethlehem's on the first Christmas night: "There is no room." Not angrily nor rudely is it turned away, but simply as an inconvenience to be set aside as a matter of course without another thought.

And God had prepared it for the soul He loved, as a precious link in its chain of graces! O divine Patience, how long will it bear with us? We would not reject, much less shatter the gift of a friend, carefully adapted to our need. And have we no remorse for defeating an eternal design, not once only, but perhaps many times in the day? He sets Himself to readjust His plan, to repair the broken links, and though He can no longer suffer, we remember that no heart has ever felt like His the pangs of unrequited love. St. Paul reminds us that He with whom we treat now is "Jesus, yesterday, today, and the same for ever," as sensitive, tender, and affectionate as with His friends of long ago, as solicitous for our welfare and the full realisation of His designs for us as ever: "Extinguish not the Spirit," the Apostle says to us. "Grieve not the holy Spirit of God whereby you are sealed, the searcher of hearts, who helpeth our infirmity, and seeing that we know not what we should pray for as we ought, and what He desireth, Himself asketh for us with unspeakable groanings…according to God."

(2)

"The Master is come and calleth for thee."—John 11:28

It was the call of Love. *"She, as soon as she heard, riseth quickly and cometh to Him."* Mary did not know what awaited her, the glorious response there would be to that obedience.

Neither do we know what God has in store for us when we rise quickly and follow His call. It is always the call of Love. In sorrow it is the call of sympathy. Her Lord waited for her to mingle His tears with hers. Had she chosen to remain at home, shut up in her own grief, or in the unhelpful company of creatures, what she would have missed! The call of the Creator is always to joy. But not always at once. There must be faith in Him and trust and love. That call is *a test*.

At times the call is to sacrifice. It was this later to His dear Magdalen. Not only when in her faithful love she followed Him to Calvary and clung to Him to the last. There at least He was with her. Not only when the tomb shut Him away from her ministrations, nor when the cloud stooped down on Olivet and took Him from her sight. She had His footprints. But during the lonely years at Ste. Baume when, according to tradition, she had to live on her memories of Him and her hope of rejoining Him again one day. And meantime to content herself with the Real but Hidden Presence which was at once her consolation and the intensifying of her desire.

We are like her in our calls to joy, to sacrifice, and to reward—always, always, to final joy: "Come, blessed of My Father!" His love has many disguises, but trustful love can see through them all. It takes a little patience. Sometimes it is our very tears that hinder our recognition of Him. They blind us so that we fail to see Him. He is close at hand, but we take Him for the gardener. It will need His call to us by name that we may know how near He has been to us all the time and how pleased to see our search for Him. Had Magdalen known they were playing "Hide and Seek" in the gaiety of that Resurrection morning, how she would have smiled through her tears!

We must learn to wait, to bide His time, ready to follow quickly whenever and whithersoever He calls.

(3)

"And He said: Come"—Matt. 14:29

"*The boat in the midst of the sea was tossed by the waves for the wind was contrary.*" It was a wild night. Contrary winds soon roused the wrath of that little inland sea. And the terror of Peter's crew increased as a figure walking upon the waves was seen approaching them. "They cried out for fear. And immediately Jesus spoke to them saying: It is I, fear ye not. And Peter making answer said: Lord, if it be thou, bid me come to thee upon the waters. And he said: Come."

How instantaneously the Heart of Christ responds to trust! There was no need for giving that obedience. What Peter asked was an unheard-of miracle, possible indeed to the Master, presumptuous surely in the disciple. But love ignores such scruples. Those two hearts had but one thought—to be together. There was no surprise at feeling the tossing waves firm beneath his feet as Peter stepped out upon them; no fear till, roused by the alarm from the boat, he turned from Jesus to look at the huge oncoming wave. Then he began to sink and cry. And his Master to reproach—not for the distraction, but for the "little faith."

There are two lessons for us in Peter's cry. We see a magnificent venture of faith and trust. But no less is there a lesson of prudence: "If it be Thou." He would be sure of the Will of God. That known, he would dare anything. Or, rather, there could be no risk.

When we are engaged in a fixed state, and conscious of a vocation—for all have a vocation—we may face without fear obstacles apparently insurmountable. It may seem impossible, but Jesus is Master of the impossible; with His help, in His strength, we shall walk upon the waters.

If we are not sure of His Will, we must beg Him to call us distinctly, and meantime must wait and pray. Without some indication of His Will it would be imprudent and presumptuous, even sinful, to endanger the life of the soul, or to embark on enterprises involving others. But as soon as from the lips of Jesus we hear "Come!" we may go forward with confidence, certain that Jesus will make safe, even easy, the way to which He calls us; for heaven and earth will pass away but His word will not pass. Those who at the Master's invitation brave peril for His sake must not question the power their trust gives them over the Sacred Heart. It cannot suffer harm to touch them so long as their eyes are fixed on Him.

All the glory of the Catholic Church, her interior holiness and their works for their fellow men, which are the admiration of all ages, are due to the ventures of her children, to the trust with which they respond to that invitation "Come!" and cast themselves into His arms who calls them. God's heroes, and notably the founders of Religious Orders, are one and all heroic by the confidence in God exemplified in their own spiritual life and in the marvellous works which their faith and trust achieve. "Let them trust in Thee who know Thee," says the Church in the words of David, words on which so many of England's convert clergy, her "modern martyrs," are building daily.

And now—what follows? If the call of a friend demands response, what must be the answer to the Creator's call?

Even from inanimate things God expects acknowledgment. "The stars were called, and they said, Here we are, and with cheerfulness they have shined forth to Him that made them."[1] Shall those to whom He has given free-will for co-operating with Him be less eager! Is a cheerful shining forth of my life to Him my answer to His call to *me?*

We can hardly read the *Acts of the Apostles* without being struck by the childlike docility with which they and their converts obeyed the inspirations of the Holy Spirit: "Go with them, nothing doubting," was said to Peter with an order from which his Jewish instincts evidently recoiled—the opening of the Christian Church to the Gentiles. Our ways are prepared by the same Divine Wisdom that guided the Prince of the Apostles in an hour of crisis. We must be guided by Him all life through if we would not go astray.

There are moments in our lives when we are face to face with a decision on which our happiness in this life and very possibly in the next may depend. With all earnestness must we then turn to God for guidance: "Teach me to do Thy Will…. Make the way known to me wherein I should walk…. Speak, Lord, for Thy servant heareth." He can hear no prayer more acceptable to Him, and those whose sincere desire is to know His Will in the critical steps of life may be sure He will direct and bless their choice. Yet how many reckless and irrevocable deeds are done—and not by unbelievers only—without so much as a passing reference to Him!

---
1 Bar. 3:35

But not only in difficult situations should we turn to our best Friend. Often during the day by loving word or thought our hearts should seek Him.

Some little children heard at Catechism that it is God who speaks to our hearts, bidding us do or not do this or that:

"I never hear Him speak to me," said one.

"Oh, don't you?" exclaimed another, in surprise, "I often do."

Why should we take for granted that God will never ask me to do great things for Him? To help one soul to salvation, to instruct one little child, is a grace I could never deserve, but if I hold myself in readiness, He may deign to call me: "Why stand you here all the day idle? Go you also into My vineyard."

When least expected, in the midst of excitement and pleasure, the whisper may come: "I have somewhat to say to thee." It was when Simon the Pharisee, after inviting our Lord to his table, had received Him with such cold hospitality, and resented His forgiveness of Magdalen, that he heard those gracious words. What an opportunity was here! Did it meet with goodwill and open a proud heart to the rebuke so meekly given? We are not told, but we know from our own experience the gentleness and patience of His dealings with ourselves:

"Behold, I stand at the door and knock. If any man shall hear My voice and open to Me the door, I will come in to him and will sup with him and he with Me." *Any man*—Could invitation be more winning? Year after year He will stand at a door and knock, offer His grace, and if repulsed, meekly retire, returning after a while, His design readjusted to meet the new situation. More marvellous, surely, than the triumphs of His power is the miracle of His patience!

It would be a sad mistake and take the heart out of much noble endeavour to restrict the term or idea of "vocation" to the call of God to the Priesthood or the Religious State, the sense in which the word is most frequently used. We have every one of us a work in life by which God invites us to serve Him and deserve eternal reward. Did we understand the glory and the happiness of this commission, our one desire would be to ascertain it and realize it as fully as possible. What! the choice of God from all eternity *of me*, a part assigned by Him to me in His universal plan, a service to Himself which because of His love for me He will accept from no other, is not this a destiny to satisfy the most extravagant ambition!

Our one desire when we meet Him in the moment of death and see the pierced Hands stretched out to us, will be—to have *satisfied* Him. By what road we have reached Him will matter little so long as we have done His Will. This, then, must be our main concern. To have *now* the listening ear that recognizes His Voice quickly and follows it gladly, will be to walk through life securely and be helpful to many on the way.

X

Trust in His Tests

(III) His Promises to Prayer

PRAYER, as the expression of Trust, naturally finds place in these pages, but why under "Tests"?

Because it *is* a test—in many cases it is the supreme test:

"I have not seen you at the usual Mass for some time," says a boy to his chum.

"I don't go now; I've left school," is the answer.

The other knows what that means.

St. Alphonsus asks the cause of the division of the human family at the Last Day; of the difference, radical and final, in the lot of each class throughout eternity. And his answer is this:

"These prayed—those did not."

It is not a question of race, circumstances, temperament, temptation. These influences, favourable and unfavourable, will be found on both sides. The cause lies much deeper:

"These prayed—the others did not."

Prayer is a subject too vast and too high to be entrusted to unskilled hands. Under two aspects, however, as a privilege and as a test one may perhaps venture to approach it.

A young missionary from Africa stood in the pulpit of a London church facing a fashionable congregation. He had been sent to Europe to plead for his black Christians, whose church, with its poor furniture, had been destroyed by fire. His quest had not been a success, and this was his last appeal. The irresponsive faces before him showed but too plainly their consciousness of being "in for another charity sermon," so, forestalling the objection: "We are not interested in Foreign Missions," he said:

"I know you have many and urgent claims nearer home. The land from which I come you hardly know by name. I can scarcely expect you to be interested in our misfortunes and our needs. And yet"—with a strong effort he controlled his voice—"and yet, I *ask you* to be interested; *do please* be interested."

Perhaps that young preacher's misgiving is shared by more than one who has to plead for Prayer. So few will be interested. "It will be urged," people will say, "as a duty, and there will be complicated rules, increasing the difficulty of what was hard to begin with. In any case, it will be most uninteresting."

Complications may be dispensed with if Faith, a most satisfactory substitute, takes their place. She brings her own retinue and rubrics. She speaks *and we are interested.* And she is so bright-faced and persuasive that we are willing to come to terms: *Sola fides sufficit;* we have the word of the Church for it. So let us take her for our guide in her twofold presentation of Prayer as Privilege and Test.

That Prayer is necessary for all who have come to the use of reason, needs no proof. It is necessary because God has so ordained. Without His grace we cannot perform one single action which will help us to gain heaven. And unless we pray, the grace of God will not be given us. He does indeed bestow His grace upon all men, for it is His Will that all should be saved. Hence He gives to all sufficient grace, which if used aright, will win those efficacious graces that lead to final perseverance. We use one of the very first graces when we pray. If we do not pray, this grace, like the seed by the wayside, is trodden down and yields no fruit. If we pray, additional grace will be given us; the more prayer, the more grace. He who prays best and most is surest of gaining eternal life; to him who prays little, less grace is given; those who pray not at all will never see the light of heaven, unless the prayers of others are in God's goodness accepted for them.

Prayer a Privilege.—But this Prayer which is so supremely necessary for us is also the grandest of privileges. To enhance a boon and at the same time forestall excuse, royalty will issue its invitation by way of command. So does the King of kings. He knows that His worship, which is our main duty, is also our most vital need. Therefore Prayer is the first of His Commandments. But He makes Himself so accessible and gracious that perversity must be stubborn indeed not to see privilege in the command. Yet how many there are who in the freedom and familiarity of their Father's house complain of their obligation—complain when thousands would welcome the permission to eat of the crumbs that fall from their table!

It is faith, stronger faith, we lack to show us our need and the infinite resource we have in prayer. To look at it in this light is to be prepared for difficulties. And why not merge the duty in the privilege! Duty, unfortunately, does not always attract. There are some whom the very word repels, but privilege excites desire, even envy.

We might have thought of our God as unwilling to be importuned by us except on rare occasions and at distant intervals. The Lord of Infinite Majesty and of countless worlds might have deemed it an irreverence to be approached by His little creatures unless for matters of the very gravest import. Once a year, perhaps, or at time of crisis in our lives, He might have permitted us to present our needs before Him. How those times would have been prized! What care would have been taken to prepare our petitions, to make the most of our hour of audience and bring into it any and every business that by any plea could be thought deserving of His notice.

Oh, blessed be the Lord our God that He is not One such as this! That the Name He Himself puts upon our lips when we speak to Him is "Father," a name inviting—nay, exacting—the love and the trust of a child. We are to come to Him whenever we will, the oftener the better. We may ask what we will and as often as we will, the more we ask, the better will He be pleased. We may come again and again and be importunate and insatiable, and we are welcome always. The most self-seeking petition and the most disinterested praise find Him always ready, interested and understanding. All my interests and my troubles, the secrets of my inner life with its hopes and fears, and the varying moods that affect my intercourse with Him, my efforts and my falls; my home life, too, with its responsibilities, difficulties and family trials, my pleasures and my pains, all may be poured out freely before Him. With perfect frankness and confidence my heart may speak, counting upon His counsel and help. Is there anything I cannot say to my Father and my Friend, any event great or small for which I may not expect His sympathy? He never tires of the same old story which must try the endurance of my most indulgent listener.

Was it not Fr. de Ravignan who gave this counsel: "In your dealings with others be yourself without your faults," that is, be natural, don't try to imitate someone else. "In dealing with Almighty God we can improve upon this by the omission of three letters: 'be yourself *with* your faults.' We ought to come before Him just as we are, with all our faults about us, no pretences, no excuses, glad He should see what He does see, my inmost self through and through and through. Nothing teaches us confidence in God like this taking of our faults to Him in perfect sincerity. He loves to be trusted with all that concerns us, especially with our weaknesses and our sins. We come from converse with Him such as this, relieved, refreshed, peaceful and true."

How earnestly that young missionary pleaded for the interest of those to whom he was appealing! He knew that *there* lay his only hope of success—their interest in the souls of others, of strangers. Can there be less need of interest, *our* interest in our own soul? It is all we need in order to pray, really pray. "Work out your salvation," says St. Paul. The very words tell of keen interest, of a task requiring thought, care, perseverance. We talk of working out a sum, not expecting it to come right of itself. If I am thoroughly interested in the great work for which I am sent into this world, I shall pray. Do I find it hard to ask for what I *really* want?

Our Lord tells us that our heart is with our treasure. If my hope and my heart are in heaven, earthly ambitions, excitements and pleasures will not draw away my heart from God. I shall not envy the slight percentage of mankind who enjoy the fruits of success in this life. I may pray for success, for health and happiness, for peace and plenty, for deliverance from the ills of life, but it will be without the feverish activity of those whose hearts are wholly set on the things of this life. Nor, on the other hand, shall I give way to discontent if I have to plod along till death in weariness or pain.

No sincere prayer is lost. Not a sigh of my heart is overlooked. Every request I make is heard, not always at the time I expect nor in the way I desire, because my Father knows what will be harmful, and what will be for my good, and in His Wisdom He withholds the one and bestows the other. Supernatural gifts and graces which will enrich us with treasures that neither sickness nor death can take away—these He will always give. Sin alone can really harm me, and if I pray aright, no sin will hold me, no temptation be too strong for me, no trial cast me down. The Christian who prays may say with the Apostle: "I can do all things in Him who strengthens me."

Our Lord is our Teacher in prayer. He would trust this instruction to no other. In the *Our Father* He teaches us the objects of our prayer and the order of our petitions. As our Elder Brother He has brought us into a new relationship with the Eternal Father, more familiar, more tender than any that had gone before. Hence in prayer the interests of our Heavenly Father, His worship, praise and thanksgiving must come first; then provision for ourselves. Are we not apt to invert this order, so far as to confine our prayers almost exclusively to petition?

Two friends, a Catholic and a Protestant, passing a church in London, the Catholic said:

"I should like to go in here for a few minutes; will you come?"

"I don't mind; you won't be long, I suppose."

Five minutes and they were out again on the pavement.

"I thought you were never coming out. What on earth were you saying all that time?"

"I was asking for what I want. What do *you* say when you kneel down to pray?"

"Say?…God bless my wife and children, of course; what else is there to say?"

Simply as creatures of God there would be much else. But as Catholics we have in the Communion of Saints a great deal more. Christ our Lord as King of this world has chosen to associate His subjects with Him in the degree wherein they have His interests at heart. By the

Apostleship of Prayer which the Pope would desire to see all join, we have an easy and efficacious means of uniting in a world-wide league of intercession for all the interests of the Sacred Heart. Our responsibilities as Catholics do not begin and end with our own family or parish, or even with our own country, for in every part of the world we have an opportunity of promoting the cause of God's Church for His honour and glory. Our interests may be as wide as the Church herself. I look at a crucifix, at the parched lips and the outstretched arms. Where is there a soul on earth I may not lift to those thirsting lips and draw into the shelter of that embrace!

Among the many familiar objects of prayer, I may single out specially at this critical time the conversion of England; the sore distress of multitudes tossed to and fro by every wind of doctrine; her married clergy, many of them reduced with their families to actual poverty by their conversion; the children lost to the Church as the result of mixed marriages; the Catholic children, whose parents never go to Mass. We may go round the world praying for the interests of our Lord in the various countries, those especially where Religion is persecuted. For the fifteen hundred millions of the world's population; the thousands upon thousands who live and die without knowledge of the true God; the eighty thousand who die daily, many of them overtaken by sudden death; the numbers in mortal sin. For our own unemployed and suffering poor. For our Government and all who control the interests of our country and of the world. For the peace of the world and harmony among the nations.

Among all the gifts that He has lavished on us is there a greater than this unrestricted, familiar intercourse with Himself of "the eternal King of worlds,"[1] "our God who is present to all our petitions"?[2] Should we not try to realize that the *privilege* of Prayer is the character which dominates all others, that duty and necessity are not only included but lost in it, as is serfdom in sonship? Many things which claim our prayers now we shall want no more in Heaven. But the privilege of its prayer which will then be all Praise will be our portion for ever. Meanwhile, it has another aspect and so long as we are *in via* we must be prepared for the experience of finding.

Prayer a Test.—With rare exceptions our intercourse with God is more or less laborious and difficult. The raising up of the mind and heart to Him is a supernatural action involving supernatural acts, impossible without help from above. It is hard to keep up attention for any length of time, distractions pour in from every side and it is weary work fighting against them. There is difficulty, then, from the nature of prayer itself, and we must be prepared for it. Otherwise, discouragement will supervene and sooner or later prayer will be given up.

Our way to Heaven depends on two things: the grace of God and our co-operation. His action upon the soul is always at hand, but our will is often sluggish. Because of their intimate relation and reaction on one another, body and soul are continually at variance, the soul as mistress

---

1 Tobias 13:6
2 Deut. 4:7

dictating, the handmaid resenting the impulse given and the restraint involved.

For Prayer must have certain qualities, among which one holds pre-eminence and almost includes the rest. Perhaps there is nothing in Scripture more insisted on than the reverence with which the Majesty of God must be approached. It appears in the ceremonial that surrounded the Tabernacle in the wilderness. It is the very atmosphere of the Heavenly Court: St. John, in a glimpse of Heaven, the Home of perfect freedom, shows the reverence of the rubrics there. And most strikingly it was taught by our Lord Himself as soon as He came amongst us.

Speaking of Him as our Model in prayer, St. Paul says: "*He was heard for His reverence.*"[1] Wonderful words when we remember who He is and on how many grounds He had a right to be heard. Was there no stronger plea on which His prayer might rest—the dignity of His Person! "whereas He was the Son of God in whom the Father is well pleased"? And His merits? Surely such claims might have been fittingly urged. But these He could not share with His brethren, and in a matter so vital as the conditions for acceptable prayer, it behooved Him to set an example all can follow.

What are we that we should be heard? Unprofitable servants at the best. And our dispositions, what are they? But reverence is in the power of every one of us, saint and sinner alike; it is precisely the sense of sin and unworthiness that should make reverence a necessity to us.

In our Lord's prayer beneath the olive trees the night

---
1 Heb. 5:7

before His Passion, all the characteristics of perfect prayer are found. But it is reverence that is singled out for special notice: "He fell upon His Face, praying." There was intensity of entreaty: "With a strong cry and tears He offered up prayers and supplications to Him that was able to save Him from death." There was fortitude: "And being in an agony He prayed the longer." There was perseverance: " The second time He went and prayed.... And He prayed the third time saying the self-same word." There was perfect resignation: "If it be possible let this chalice pass from me; nevertheless, not as I will but as Thou wilt." All the requisites for perfect prayer are here. But we are distinctly told, "He was heard *for His reverence.*"

With all our shortcomings and unworthiness, which of us can say this is a condition beyond our power to provide? For some of us, perhaps, it may be the only recognised excellence we can bring. Our prayer may have no fervour, no sustained attention worth speaking of, but who will dare own to *irreverence?*

The world is doing its best to stamp out reverence from the hearts of children, for God, for parents, for all in authority, for law. Let us teach them in the happy years of innocence—teach, above all, by example, what we must all learn if we are to be admitted to the Home of our Father who is in Heaven, to the Court of the King of kings:

"And every creature which is in heaven, and on the earth, and under the earth, and such as are in the sea.... I heard all saying: To Him that sitteth on the throne and to the Lamb benediction and honour and glory and power for ever and ever. Amen.... And they fell down before the throne upon their faces and adored Him that liveth for ever and ever."[1]

This is what St. John saw in Heaven. And what do the Blessed in Heaven see upon earth in too many of us when we come to pray before "the tabernacle of God with men"? Must not levity of mind and manner to the Heavenly Court be inexplicable? Might it not help us to come more fittingly before that tabernacle were we to lift our eyes and hearts for a moment to the worship going on above us just within the veil? So close is the alliance between body and soul, that the attitude and action of one has its immediate influence upon the other. What if some failing here should account in part for unanswered prayer, if a grace long withheld should be the reward at last of a closer following of the Master who was *"heard for His reverence"*!

The Church is a trainer in reverence. Of Father de Ravignan it was said that in the pulpit of Notre Dame his sermon was preached when he had made *his* Sign of the Cross.

The persistence of distractions is the great and general complaint of us all. Is there no remedy? None that proves altogether effective. St. Bernard bade his wandering thoughts stay outside the church door and await his coming out; but there is no record of their obedience. Hearing that St. Aloysius had resolved to spend an hour in undistracted prayer, a boy remarked: "He must have been awfully glad when he got near the end of the time!" But there is help, if not remedy, for goodwill, and within the reach of us all:

---

1 Apoc. 5:13

> "A roving mind and a faithful heart
> May go together,
> Like the straying clouds and the steadfast sky
> In stormy weather."

One of our modern medicines is thus advertised on the bottles: "These tabloids of compressed phenacetin possess many advantages.... They are extensively prescribed for business men, travellers, and others, as the compact form of the medicine enables the patient to take the dose regularly without interfering with his ordinary avocations."

Now the change of three words provides an excellent spiritual advertisement: "These forms of compressed Prayer (Aspirations) possess many advantages. They are extensively prescribed for business men, travellers, and others, as the compact form of the medicine enables the patient to take the dose regularly without interfering with his ordinary avocations." Notice that we all come under one or other of the classes provided for: we are all patients—sick, some of one disease, some of another; all business people—or ought to be—our heads and hearts full of the one thing necessary, the laying up treasure for heaven; and at any rate, all travellers who have here no lasting city but are hastening forward to one or two eternities.

We contrive to meet every need when there is question of keeping up our bodily strength. But does the soul find the like attention? There are the Sacraments, of course, and daily Mass, and prayers morning and night. But what about our toilers with little time for anything but the business that fills every cranny of the day? Is there no spiritual restorative or refreshment always at hand that can be taken at all times and in all places—going up and down stairs, on a doorstep, whilst waiting for a visitor, a tonic repairing the soul's strength without any great effort or tiring application of mind or interference with work?

Yes, there are aspirations or ejaculations. Aspiration, i.e. *breathing towards*, expresses desire. An aspirant for honours in an examination is one who has set his heart on coming out grandly in a test. Aspirations are the breathings of the soul towards God—short acts of love, of trust, of resignation to His Will, that escape from it as easily, as softly as the breath, and rise to Him. Ejaculations, or *darts*, express the same thing in a different way. As a dart flies suddenly and swiftly, and has done its work before any hindrance can stop it, so the loving prayer or desire has been darted forth from the heart and reached our Heavenly Father before the devil has had time to turn it aside. And thus it comes to pass that those whose longer prayers are full of distractions can make up for shortcomings by these frequent acts. They are strongly recommended by all the masters of prayer who tell us they help greatly to obtain from God that grace which we should desire above all others—the spirit of Prayer.

Who cannot rouse himself to say with all his heart:

"My God, I love Thee, teach me to love Thee more!"
"Eternal rest give to them, O Lord!"
"Thy Kingdom come!"
"Heart of Jesus, in Thee I trust!"

Or in the helpful words of Scripture:

"I know in whom I have believed."
"I do believe, help Thou my unbelief!"
"How long dost Thou turn away Thy Face from me?"
"Hear me speedily for I am in trouble!"
"O Lord, give ear to my tears!"
"Let my cry find a hiding-place in Thee!"

There is no rule to be followed. If we love God these breathings of love will come as it were spontaneously. If we want to love Him more, they will teach us. All circumstances will suggest them—temptation, the sight of abject poverty, a church, the song of a bird, the sea, a sudden joy or trouble, toothache, almost anything. We can quickly learn the art of making everything—our failings above all things—stepping stones to rise to God.

The Church has provided a whole treasury of indulgenced aspirations. What a pity to lose such an easy way of glorifying God and helping the living and the dead! When the suffrages of the Church are dealt out in Purgatory, let it not be our lot to be passed over because in our day we had sent little or no help to the Holy Souls. Knowing how easily we lose sight of the supernatural, the Church seeks at Mass to recall wandering thoughts on entering the Canon: "*Sursum Corda!* Lift up your hearts," she cries. And we—as if resenting a quite unnecessary admonition—reply: "*Habemus ad Dominum,* We *have* them lifted up to the Lord!"

Before prayer she would have us make a good start by reverently calling to mind the Presence of God; patiently recall wandering thoughts when we advert to them; and then trust the result to God. We are not to be at the mercy of our fitful moods, nor disconcerted at long spells of dryness and inertness. A boy thus defined weather and climate: "Weather only lasts a short time; climate lasts all the time." Some of us find more climate than weather in our spiritual course. Apparently Father de Ravignan was of the number. It was with the persuasiveness of experience that he spoke of "the courage of prayer" and of the vigorous effort needed to make the plunge. Speaking of the resolution with which he faced seasons of spiritual trial, his biographer says that, like a traveller overtaken by fog or storm of wind and sleet, he wrapped his cloak closer about him, breasted the blast, and quickened his pace.

> When Prayer delights thee least
> Then learn to say
> "Soul, now is greatest need
> That thou shouldst pray!"

"Your Father knoweth," is our Lord's consolation to us in time of trial, and it is enough. He knows that prayer is hard to most people; and often good-will is all that He asks, accepting, we are told, "a great deal of what may be called formal service from His servants." *Devotion* not *emotion* is what He looks for—not tenderness of feeling which we cannot always command, but readiness of will in what belongs to His service, though it may have little warmth of affection to offer. Devotion clings fast to the good pleasure of God, through distractions, difficulties and darkness, as loyalty to a leader is never deeper and more devoted than in the hour of trial and sacrifice. "She hath done what she could," was our Lord's grateful acknowledgment of Magdalen's service. A servant of God was wont to say: "God's praise which is the repose of Heaven has to be a sacrifice on earth."[1] The reward hereafter is gained here. When the heir, arrived at maturity, looks back upon the various stages of his education and notes their effect upon his mind and character, he can appreciate the experiences through which, by the appointment of the father, he has had to pass.

"Bring everything, change everything into prayer," says Father de Ravignan, "pains, trials, temptations of all kinds—*pray* in the calm, *pray* in the storm, *pray* on awaking, *pray* during the day—tired out and distracted, *pray*, whatsoever your repugnance, *pray*; *pray* that you may learn to pray."

St. Teresa said she would answer for the salvation of anyone who would make a quarter of an hour's mental prayer daily. It was a bold promise, but the prudent saint knew she was safe.

In His instructions and parables there are few things on which our Blessed Lord insists more earnestly than on the necessity and the value of persevering prayer. He stops at nothing when He would bring home to us its power with God. With divine daring He creates situations, implies comparisons, assumes characters we should have thought inadmissible—an unjust judge who only hears the cause of a poor widow, "lest coming continually she weary me"; a disobliging neighbour who objects to being disturbed at midnight by a friend in need, but rises at last and gives

---

1 Mère Marie de Jésus, Carmelite, 1853-1917

all that is wanted, not because the troubler is a friend, our Lord adds, but because he *continues* knocking.

See how He Himself invites and rewards persistence:

He had retired into the coasts of Tyre and Sidon and "would that no man should know it." The evangelist does not say He hid from one who in sore need was following Him, crying: "Have mercy on me, O Lord, Thou Son of David, my daughter is grievously troubled by a devil." Yet—"He answered her not a word…. The disciples besought Him, saying: Send her away for she crieth after us." As if to avoid her, He went into a house by the way. But she came in and fell down at His feet, saying: "Lord, help me!" Then He spoke, but only to say He had come for Israel, not for her; it was not meet to take the children's bread and cast it to the dogs. "Yea, Lord," was the quick retort, "for the whelps also eat of the crumbs that fall from the table of their masters." The disciples were amazed at her audacity. She was braving Him. Had she no fear? But His Face was aglow with admiration. She had shown herself "strong against God," and He owned Himself vanquished. "O woman, great is thy faith, be it done to thee as thou wilt; go thy way, the devil is gone out of thy daughter." St. Matthew and St. Luke tell the story. It is St. Luke who adds: "And He said to her: *For this saying* go thy way"—her last fearless words had won her cause.

Had she gone away discouraged, who could have blamed her? But what a loss it had been to her and to thousands with her! For our sakes Christ has made that heathen woman, like a Roman centurion, a teacher of prayer to all time.

In His familiar instructions and parables our Lord was constantly noting the analogy there is between the natural and the supernatural worlds. His lessons were drawn from the homely scenes of village life and from the little ones He loved to have about Him. A like analogy exists in our own day. The only question is: Do illustrations borrowed from twentieth century life and manners jar upon our sense of fitness? Eastern scenes and ways are a setting the effect of which is due in great part to their associations. Do the commonplaces of our comfort-loving age, when utilised for the exposition of supernatural truths, help or harm? Let us see—the subject may be the tests in which love delights, or the power of persistent prayer, both of them lessons taught by our Lord's treatment of the Syro-Phœnician woman:

A man sits at his breakfast table, his attention divided between his morning paper and his toast:

Presently there is a voice at his side:

"Da, give me some toast." No answer, not even the lifting of an eye from the paper. After a pause it comes again:

"Please, Da, give me some toast." No answer, and a longer pause.... Then once more:

"Please, Da, give May some toast."

"I think May's a shabby little beggar."

"Please, Da, give May, shabby little beggar, some toast."

She got the toast.

We can alter May's pleading to suit our own needs: "Lord, help me in this difficulty and trouble."

His Promises to Prayer

No answer comes. "Do please, Lord, help me, for no one else can, and I have prayed so long." Should He answer: "I know you, and you know yourself to be undeserving of any favour." "Please, dear Lord, do give me, undeserving as I am, what I trustfully ask, relying on Your promises to prayer." Sooner or later the answer will come:

"Be it done to thee as thou wilt."

God has His conditions certainly, and these I must accept. I am His child. What I ask may not always be the best for me. And though He hears unfailingly, He does not always reply immediately. The answer may come after years of waiting, but no reminder of my trust in Him will ever be lost in the distance or forgotten. To Him I may confide every sorrow, every need. To Him I may fly for protection and help, not at set times only but at every turn. Always ready for me and glad to see me, never wearied by the same old story, He welcomes me in proportion to my demands upon Him and to my importunity. His reproach is not that I want so much and so often, but that I ask for so little. For thirty years Monica prayed and wept for the conversion of her Augustine from error and sin. What marvellous conversions sought for during a lifetime have been granted only at the eleventh hour! For hundreds of years we have been praying with chosen souls of other lands for the conversion of England. We must pray on; pray with perseverance; prayer prevails at last. One who denied the omnipotence of prayer said: "If any man prayed earnestly for light it was Newman—and see where it led him!"

It is the want of trust that makes us so impatient when our prayers are not heard at once. We make a novena, and if the answer we want does not come at the end, we get discouraged and sulky like spoilt, ill-behaved children. So like, that when we find children making a novena, we take it upon ourselves to suggest to Almighty God as an additional reason for granting their request, that it is not safe to disappoint children—note the reason—they do not understand a refusal or a delay; they cannot *as yet* enter into the motives for it and will lose their confidence. An excellent argument, only the pity is we do not see the implied rebuke to ourselves! When we are not heard at once, do we say to ourselves what we say to children, come to the use of reason, that if God does not give us now all we should like to have, it is not because He grudges us anything, but because some things would harm not help us? But He has promised always to hear prayer, and if He does not give us directly the very thing we ask, He will give us something ever so much better by-and-by. When we ask for bread or a fish He will not give us a stone or a serpent. Should we in our foolishness ask for a serpent or a stone, can we be surprised if He finds something better? A wise father always reserves to himself the right of substituting a more useful gift than what the child actually wants and asks. And he expects it to understand and trust him.

Our Lord's promises to trustful prayer are simply magnificent: "Whatsoever you shall ask, believing, you shall receive." If we do not receive, it is either because we have not prayed enough, or that our faith has been at fault, or that the grant of our prayer would have harmed us, or that God has something better in store for us. It is never because the thing we ask is too difficult to obtain.

Nothing is too difficult. Who shall restrain the force of His reiterated commands and promises, or assign limits where He puts none?

"Your Father knoweth that you have need of these things. Ask...seek...knock.... For every one that asketh receiveth, and he that seeketh, findeth: and to him that knocketh, it shall be opened. Therefore, I say unto you, *all things whatsoever* you ask when ye pray, *believe* that you shall receive: and *they shall come unto you.*"

X

Trust in His Tests

(IV) His Discipline of Suffering

"They went back another way into their own country"—Matt. 2:12

THEORY and Practice—how widely parted they are in the lives of many of us! We pride ourselves on being consistent, yet fail pitiably when there is question of suffering. That there is no living in this world without pain of body and mind, that having wandered from the right path we must return to our Country by another way, and that God in His mercy has made suffering—the penalty of sin—a most powerful means of salvation and sanctification, all this we know. Yet how many make no use of this knowledge, and not only reap no benefit from suffering but turn it to their temporal or even eternal punishment hereafter! Some carry their cross to Hell, others to Purgatory, others to Heaven. Some bear it, rebelling against their lot, like the bad thief; others, like Simon of Cyrene, at first under compulsion; others, in fine, with resignation, even joy, like Christ and His saints.

His Discipline of Suffering 113

To bear our cross at least with resignation is necessary if we are to be true Christians, i.e., followers of Christ. For "if anyone will come after Me," says our Lord, "let him deny himself and take up his cross and follow Me."

The temper of mind that will admit of no consolation either from heaven or earth in the agony of its grief, is simple rebellion. It was the temper of the impenitent thief who closed his eyes to the example of the divine Sufferer at his side, and his heart to the pleadings of grace that had won the heart of his companion. He would receive comfort in one shape only—instantaneous freedom from the pain that tortured him. This is the cross-bearing that condemns instead of saving. We are meant to be humbled and softened by the Cross, not embittered. We are to turn to our Heavenly Father for the consolation He will surely give us, for the strength to prove ourselves worthy of the test which the Cross brings. A cross borne merely by compulsion may lead to rebellion, abiding estrangement from God and eternal ruin. Accepted with just sufficient submission to avoid sin by murmuring or morbid self-pity, is scarcely more than cross-dragging, a less generous but not an easier way: our Lord deserves more loyal service than this.

At the baptismal font God made us His sons and heirs, on condition that when able to answer for ourselves we should ratify the promises made in our name. We are expected to act then as we do on choosing a profession or occupation. We apply to an expert to be instructed and kept up to the mark. Two short words of St. Paul sum up our glorious heritage as co-heirs with Christ, and our obligations: "*Yet so if we suffer with Him,*" he says. "*Yet so.*" Therefore the Providence of God is careful to secure to us our title-deeds, to give us the wherewith to fill up in ourselves those things that are wanting in the sufferings of Christ—the small pains He has left for us to make our election sure.

That unalloyed happiness is the earthly reward of a good life, and that trust in God will guard us from every sorrow, is a mistake against which the Church is ever seeking to protect her children. She bids us pray, "so to pass through the good things of time as not to lose those of eternity," and would have us *ask* "to be prepared for the rewards to come." Rewards are prizes for well-doing, especially for efforts that have entailed pain and persevering labour. To be prepared for reward is to be put in the way of tasks that involve a certain amount of courage and endurance. Does this look as if she regards the trials of this life, and the more testing vicissitudes of the spiritual life, as evils, and not rather as pledges of God's presence with us and favour? To refuse preparation for reward, is it not to reject the prize?

Are not the noblest lives recorded in history those which so far from shirking toil and suffering have courted them as providing the means for a fuller service of God and a closer following of Christ? Of such He Himself has said: "The Kingdom of heaven suffereth violence and the violent bear it away."

So have the martyrs of all time regarded them. The Apostles, scourged, stoned, crucified, rejoiced that they were accounted worthy to suffer for the name of Jesus. And the martyrs of our own land, from the days of Henry

VIII to Emancipation. And after Emancipation, those "living martyrs" who in our own times are renouncing for themselves and for their children the good things of time that they may not lose those of eternity. Not in Mexico only, or under the burning skies of Africa, or in the leper settlements throughout the world, but in many a hidden home, perhaps at our very doors, are men and women leading heroic lives, welcoming the daily sacrifices which liken them to their suffering Saviour, and with a generosity known to God alone, proving their loyalty to Him.

On the lips of even her frail children the Church puts the same prayer: "That Thou wouldst not forsake us but wouldst prepare us for the rewards to come." And they—or some of them—no sooner see the least sign of such preparation, than they cry out in despair that the Lord has forgotten them. Truly we are hard to satisfy!

A further reason for trial and probation here on earth is this:

Divine Love, like our feeble imitation of it, has its tests. Before admitting to the face to face Vision of Himself, God submits His intelligent creatures to proof. All around Him in His heavenly Court are proven ones: "They that are with Him are called elect and faithful," "who might have transgressed and did not transgress." Angels were tried. And we who are made a little lower than the angels are, like them, to win our crowns by way of reward. "Fear not, for God is come to prove you,"[1] are amongst the earliest words of God to His chosen people. In his distress David prayed:

---
1 Exod. 20:20

"Prove me, O Lord, and try me."[1] Thus, even in the Old Law, to be proved by trial was accounted a mark of divine favour. After the sufferings and death of Christ, the Cross, as might be expected, plays a still more prominent part in God's training of His elect. For some it is comparatively light. Others, like our forefathers in England under persecution, have to carry a very heavy and lifelong cross. But we have one and all to remember that having wandered from the right path, we have to reach our country by another way, "the King's Highway of the Holy Cross."

What, then, is the cross, our own cross, on the bearing of which so much depends?

By the cross we mean whatever in our lives is painful to nature; whatever in times of exceptional trial, in daily duties, in our intercourse with others is a cause of suffering, physical or mental. All that goes against self, all that it costs to reduce self, to battle with temptation, to prefer the good pleasure of God to our own will, fatigue, monotony, disappointment in the way things fall out, all these occurrences are the portions of Christ's cross assigned *to us*. As His members we must share suffering with Him now if we want to share complete and never-ending happiness with Him by-and-by.

It is a great step on the road to heaven when we come to understand what is meant by the cross, to see the spiritual side of everyday difficulties—the reason of the perpetual annoyance we are always getting from so-and-so, of the bodily sickness which so disables us at times, the

---

[1] Ps. 25:2

anxiety we feel for those under our charge. All these little troubles, added to the big things which now and again come on us like an avalanche, are so many fragments of the cross which our Lord in His mercy lays upon us to give us a title to His rewards.

We know that whatever happens is by the Will or the permission of God. There is no such thing as chance. "All our ways are prepared." What preparation is made for a visit from royalties! What sense of responsibility appears in all officials! What vigilance to foresee all possible dangers, to see to details wherever the royal visitors are expected!

But the most elaborate provision earth has ever made is as nothing compared with the solicitude which has prepared the way of the humblest child of God. Its lot in life down to the minutest circumstance has been His care. Every influence that will tell upon it, every sorrow from the most searching trial to the slightest accident, all was foreseen from eternity and provided for by Infinite Wisdom and Infinite Love with exact adaptation to its needs.

St. Paul has some very striking words as to the way in which we are to regard our cross. "*Let us run with patience,*" he says, "*to the fight proposed to us.*" To run with energy, courage, perseverance, is a counsel we might expect. But the word of the great Apostle carries a deeper meaning—we are to run *with patience*.

Nature loves action. It will toil, it will suffer, if it may put out its powers. But inaction tries it sorely. The fray with its tortures is less formidable than the sick-bed. We seek to justify our restlessness by calling it zeal. But he who had labored more than all the apostles teaches a different lesson—that to lie still and endure may be a nobler work, a grander apostolate, a surer conquest of our enemies, a swifter advance on our way Home than the most strenuous activity of mind or body.

"Patience," St. Paul tells us, "hath a perfect work." Our desires may be good, but they must be well-regulated. We are to run, not aimlessly, but to a goal. We are to strive, not as "beating the air," but "*to the fight proposed to us.*" It may be at the front, in the sight of all, or at that part of the field where endurance is more heroic than valour. We have each our appointed post to which from all eternity the finger of God has pointed as the place where we are to labour for His glory and to win our crown. Can we desire anything better? "They also serve who only stand and wait."

How many of us need this reminder! How many run the risk of missing their vocation by refusing to recognize it at their door, in the persons, the circumstances, the anxieties, the opportunities of their daily life! We may wait, indeed, we often must wait for the full unfolding of God's designs. But we have also to bear in mind that His Will is unfolding in the happenings of every hour, and that whilst waiting we have to *serve* according to the actual light vouchsafed us. Else we may come to the end of our appointed course, and because there was no call from the heavens, no luminous star to guide us, have failed to recognize our mission. The souls we were meant to help were those of our own household or neighbourhood; occasions of glorious service were not wanting; but like the Jews of our Lord's time, we failed to see the Will of God in the signs of the times.

His Discipline of Suffering

We can only be saved by keeping the Commandments—that is, by fulfilling our duties to God, to our neighbour, and to ourselves. This requires the exercise of self-control, which in most cases amounts to self-denial. No man has any real power over himself who cannot practice self-denial. Men regarded as heroes by the world, men who have earned a great name in history, were in too many instances slaves to their passions and exhibited a moral cowardice which not religion only, but right reason, must condemn.

It is not usual to look to the Board of Trade for guidance in spiritual matters. But its President in 1922[1] gave sound advice to his fellow countrymen when he said: "Seek happiness by limiting your desires, not by gratifying them." The Catechism says plainly: "We are bound to deny ourselves because our natural inclinations are prone to evil from our very childhood and if not corrected by self-denial they will certainly carry us to hell." Hence, the first thing that we teach a child is his prayers, that from the earliest dawn of reason he may have divine help in controlling evil tendencies. Some degree of self-denial is therefore necessary in order to save our souls. No one likes it and it is not easily practiced unless we are deprived by God or voluntarily refuse ourselves somewhat more of earthly pleasures than is necessary. A very easy, very comfortable and painless life is usually out of harmony with the faithful, and still more with the generous service of God. Hence the wisdom of those who by acts of self-denial train the will to ready obedience, not only when in dangerous occasions

---

[1] Mr. Stanley Baldwin

the soul calls to "Attention!" but in minor matters also. A headache or a slight borne patiently, a grumble repressed, without being heroic deeds, may be very pleasing to God. Such acts have often led—are daily leading—men, women, even children, to the heights of sanctity. It is Father Faber who tells us that "little things on little wings lead little souls to heaven," and that

>"A single practice long sustained
>A soul to God endears."

We willingly accept voluntary sacrifice and suffering in this life in place of the grievous pains of Purgatory and as a means of obtaining His favour and grace, not for ourselves only, but, through the Communion of Saints, for a multitude of others living and dead.

A Heavy Cross.—It comes at times when we feel physically and morally unfit for any output of energy. Our cry is to be left alone, to nurse our grief in solitude. And just at this moment there is a call to action.

How nobly it was answered during the Great War! No sooner had death struck down fathers, husbands, brothers—the glory and brightness of the home—than mothers and wives, instead of giving themselves up to selfish grief, set to work to meet the needs of others, turned their homes into hospitals and devoted themselves to the tending of the sick and wounded.

"Tutors and governors by the appointment of the Father" have days of stress and anguish proved to many a soul, lifting them from mediocrity into the region of the heroic. The crisis passed and the whole aspect of life was changed. In many cases it took on a sombre aspect, uneventful, monotonous even, but satisfying by a new content and stimulating by a stronger hope. They know now what that test has been to them, what it has done for them. They recognize even now what they will see joyfully in the light of eternity—how "Thy Providence, O Father, governed" and guided it towards a determined end; how at the cost and in spite of enduring pain, it has brought them nearer to God and given them in place of earthly satisfactions His priceless gift of Peace. The heart may turn to God in its pain and the will adhere firmly to Him through conflict and desolation. This is the carrying of the Cross and the following of Christ to which His richest promises are made. It is the fellowship here which brings most intimate union and happiness hereafter.

Seasons of trial are the main tests of trust. It was trouble that brought the heavy burdened to the feet of Jesus when "He came in and went out amongst us," and shows us how He dealt with the suffering in mind or body.

By His own example our Lord teaches us how to profit by the Cross: "Watch and pray." Both are necessary in life's daily troubles as in its crucial hours. From the first step of resignation and patience to the highest which welcomes the Cross for Christ's sake, there must be prayer.

We could hardly have thought of the Son of God offering Himself as our example here, praying in bitterest distress to His Father, with whom He has one undivided Nature and is equal in all things. Yet how could He have failed us just when we need example most? Prayer is itself a test, especially when the Face of the Father seems turned away from us and His ear to be deaf to our cry. Therefore the night before His Passion our Lord withdrew from His three chosen disciples and abandoned Himself in the Garden of Gethsemane to anguish of mind and body which reduced Him to the agony of death. "And being in an agony He prayed the longer." The word supposes struggle. Was there, then, conflict in that prayer? Yes, for our consolation He allowed us to see the shrinking and terror of His human will from the torments prepared for it, and the firm adherence to the Will of the Father ever one with His own. When in our hours of anguish our will not only shrinks, but is in danger of actual antagonism to the divine Will, where should we turn for strength but to the agonizing Heart of Christ!

"*Abba, Father, if it be possible* remove this chalice," was the preface of our Lord to His prayer in the Garden. We may say this with Him in our trials, provided we add with Him: "Nevertheless, if this chalice may not pass from Me but I must drink it, Thy Will be done." Many of us are ready to say the preface; but we shrink from the "Amen" as if it were inviting trouble. As if taking advantage of our submission and trust, our Father would lay upon us more than our strength could bear. Would that be worthy of Him?

There are times when His loving designs for us will not let Him give us the things on which our hearts are set, as a father will not let his little boy who loves machinery become an engine driver, nor his little girl who loves animals become a keeper at the Zoo. He has to provide, not for our childish whims, nor always for the removal for our real trials, but for an everlasting happiness which will satisfy for eternity all our desires. "All is well," said the holy Curé of Ars, "if we carry our Cross well." And again: "It is the fear of crosses that is our greatest cross."

When danger or grave trial faces us, let us, if we can, spend in prayer like our divine Master the last moments that separate us from it. The Tabernacle where He is really present may be near at hand. Or in the solitude of our own soul we shall find Him, knowing already our story and our need, but giving us the relief of telling it.

"My God, if it be possible" shall always mean "if it be in accordance with Your Will." You are Omnipotent, the God of infinite resources, having ways of bringing things about that I cannot even guess. You can easily free me from this pain. Have pity on me and help me. But if Your Will is—not to take away this cross, but to help me to bear it; if it is necessary to the realization of your designs that through it I may be nearer to You in Heaven and love You more, then, dear Father, I take it trustfully from Your hand. Help me to bear it as You would have me, and to say from my heart with Your beloved Son: "Not my will but Thine be done."

Temptation.—Many of us would gladly be neutral in the strife between good and evil going on around and within us. Impossible. We must take a side. "I believe in peace at any price," said an American statesman in 1914, "and the price now—*is war.*" The same is true of a warfare every one of us must wage today. In greater or less degree temptation is the lot of all men; it is the "fight proposed to us," and to the soul that tries to please God it is a trial that above all others calls for patience. For on the sorrow and humiliation that follow our daily falls the enemy counts to rob us of our peace, a result well worth his efforts, should he gain nothing more. We need, then, the encouraging words of St. James: "My brethren, count it all joy when you fall into divers temptations knowing that the trial of your faith worketh patience." Like other trials, temptation is permitted by God to give us an opportunity of distinguishing ourselves. Hence we are warned: "When thou comest to the service of God, prepare thy soul for temptation." And again: "Because thou wast acceptable to God it was necessary that temptation should prove thee."

We are too apt to think that we have forfeited all claim to the loving kindness and protection of God if we have not borne a cross heroically or come unscathed out of temptation. Do we judge like this in earthly warfare? Is it not the wounded and the weary who get sympathy and care? Should we dare to discourage one who had failed somewhat in the struggle? And will our heavenly Father be less merciful to us than we are to one another? May He give us for our own soul the charity we are bound to have for others, the trust in God that turns to Him quickly in failure or relapse. No matter how much or how often we fail, He hastens at our first cry: "When thou thinkest I am far from thee I am often nearest to thee. Come to Me, child, and I will put you right again. When you fall through frailty, rise up again with greater strength than before, confiding in My more abundant grace." Oh, if this were not the character of our Heavenly Father, what would become of us!

The greatest kindness a soldier can show to a comrade marching to battle in the grip of fear is to hearten him by brave words and cheerful bearing. But would a leader dream of helping a trembler by showing *himself* broken down by terror? Yet, even to this excess of charity has the God of battles, the Strength of Martyrs stooped to help and comfort us under temptation and trial, "humbling Himself to us," as the Church says on Palm Sunday. In the Agony of the Garden we see Him staggering to His sleeping friends for a word of comfort. "For in that He Himself hath suffered and been tempted, He is able to succour them also that are tempted." "God is faithful," St. Paul reminds us, "who will not suffer you to be tempted above that which you are able." "Wherefore," says St. Peter, "let them also that suffer, according to the Will of God, commend their souls to the faithful Creator."[1]

The service of God and the following of Christ admit of an infinite number of degrees, from the earliest tending of the child's opening mind, to the full union to which St. Paul testifies when he says: "I live, now not I but Christ liveth in me...." The Apostle passes from fellowship to incorporation. Fellowship calls for loyal association, but *incorporation* for a union closer still.... As the members of the body, we have to suffer with our Head. Should we deserve the name of Christians if our life bore no resemblance to Christ's; faint, indeed, yet in some respects a likeness.

It might not have entered into His designs to suffer in His own Person. Living on earth in peace and in honour, His

---
1 Peter 4:19

simple presence amongst us as our Head would have given value to our pains. We should not have dared to represent to Him the need of example. Yet it would have lain like a load on our hearts and He would have read it there. But such restricted service of His "brethren" would have been far from contenting the generosity of the Sacred Heart. The members should not, as with us, suffer to spare the head. But the Head should suffer more than all the members for their encouragement and to give value to the little things He would leave for them to bear. So naturally did He take His place amongst us to share our lot as one of ourselves, that He could account for His frightful torments by saying simply: "Ought not Christ to have suffered *these things?*"

Comradeship is a consequence we accept as a matter of course in our compacts with one another. Even in sport we are expected to play the game. The thought that our Lord has taken as His share in the work of our redemption the death of the Cross will surely hearten us to co-operate with Him by bearing at least with patience the tribulations of this short life.

But there are those, thank God, who, not content merely to accept with resignation the trials that come, desire to be closely associated with their Lord in the endurance of pain.

As General Allenby with his troops was nearing Jerusalem, an officer noticed a Welsh soldier literally dropping from fatigue, and bade him get into an ambulance for the rest of the way. "Not with Jerusalem in front of me," was the answer, as the poor fellow pulled himself up for another effort.

His Discipline of Suffering 127

To suffer with Jesus suffering and for the intentions for which He suffered, is a motive which from the first has appealed with almost compelling force to multitudes of generous souls, even to children, as is proved by many an obscure life now being brought to light. Have we for whom He suffered as for these, any share in their ambition?

If all through life we should refuse as far as possible any fellowship with Him in suffering, how could we join in Heaven the virgin and the children martyrs, that wonderful blending of fortitude and frailty? His Court is one of infinite refinement, and the refining has been carried on in the furnace of tribulation here on earth.

"Or," you may say, "in Purgatory."

There is that alternative, but not even the fiery purification hereafter can do the work of the willingly accepted trials of this life. Every moment of such trial will add to the treasure of sanctifying grace which at the moment of death will be the measure of our eternal beatitude. To this, centuries of purgatorial suffering can bring no increase. Are not the saints wise to secure an everlasting fellowship with Christ hereafter by accepting joyfully the conditions of fellowship with Him here? The Cross is that test by which He sits refining His silver, not ruthlessly, but with exquisite discrimination of its need.

We are told that the difference between the love of Christ in Catholic and Protestant races consists mainly in this—that the Protestant dwells mainly on Christ's benefactions *to him* rather than on the need of returning on his part; the Catholic considers the sacrifice of Christ as calling for sacrifice. The instinct of Protestantism showed itself from the first; it was to abolish all that spoke of mortification or painful effort. Instead of saying with St. Paul: "I fill up what is wanting of the sufferings of Christ," it would show its appreciation of His all-sufficing satisfactions by refusing any share in them, and its loyalty by leaving Him to suffer alone. This is not the sympathy the human heart understands and values, fellowship as taught and expressed by the Catholic Church. She would have her children, crucifix in hand, watch their Saviour suffering in every fibre of His sensitive nature, in every quivering nerve—*for them*, and suffer with Him, at least, by compassion.

Many stop there. But some go further. They hear Him say: "I looked for one that would grieve together with me, but there was none; and for one that would comfort me and I found none,"[1] and there begins to stir in their hearts the desire of fellowship with Him, or saying to Him: "Where Thou art, O Lord my King, there shall Thy servant be." Beginning like Simon of Cyrene with resignation to the cross, they go on to value it, not for itself, but because of the nearness to Christ which it brings. There are those who say at last with St. Paul: "God forbid that I should glory, save in the Cross of our Lord Jesus Christ"—a wonderful protest, evincing the strength of desire in the breast of the Apostle to be likened in very deed to his suffering Lord, so far as to glory in what to a Jew would be accounted the depth of infamy.

And all the saints are with him here. Retaining their own individuality, all are conformed to the pattern on the

---
1 Ps. 118:21

Mount, prizing and welcoming every pain of soul or body which would help to conform them to Christ crucified.

How did they arrive at this height? Only by love, by personal love of Him. Holiness means likeness to Christ. We have to get this as those did who by companionship with Him on earth or by the study of Him in the Gospels have come to love Him devotedly and to form their lives on His. To His manger, to His workshop, to His retreat by night on the mountain side, they went to learn of Him. In His prayer, His suffering, His ways with others, they studied Him. For them were His costly lessons given. Echoing every one of them the words of St. Paul: "He loved me and delivered Himself *for me*," they watched Him and hung upon His words. How could they pass by heedlessly what was said and done purposely *for them*? Feebly and painfully at first, they began to tread in His footsteps, accustoming themselves to look at the hardships or difficulties or monotony of their daily life, not simply as inseparable from their circumstances and therefore inevitable, but as precious opportunities for bringing them into conformity with their Lord. They did not, they were not expected to *like* pain in itself, but they prized and loved the union and familiarity with Christ it brought about. There was an hour when for fear of having to suffer in His company those abandoned Him for whom they had left all things. And there was another hour when to follow Him even unto death they joyfully laid down their lives.

The desire of sharing sorrow with one whom we love is an instinct of our nature. If our sympathy or our companionship can be a solace to him in trial, how readily it is offered, how easy is sacrifice! The same holds good in a divine friendship. Our Lord would share with us the sharpest pain of soul and body, and those who love Him and know that sympathy with Him now is as acceptable to Him as if it had been shown on the road to Calvary long ago, welcome in their own lives those pains which are wanting in His, that cross of theirs which is a portion of His.

"*Eyes Right!*" During the Great War a picture showed an English officer marching with his men along a road of devastated Belgium. They are passing to their right a large crucifix that rises gaunt and solemn by the way, the only object left standing on that lonely scene. Suddenly the order rings out sharp:

"*Eyes Right!*" And every head turns.

To how many a desponding soul on a dreary or dangerous path has the timely "*Eyes Right!*" of a comrade led to hope and victory!

XI

Trust in His Perpetual Mediation

"Always living to make intercession for us."—Heb. 7:25

MEDIATOR is a name that should be dear to us as Saviour or Redeemer. It includes both, but is not necessarily implied in either because not essentially involving the idea of sin and propitiation. As there might have been an Incarnation without need of redemption, so in a sinless world a Mediator might have been a glorious, unsuffering link between the Creator and the creature.

How different is the reality brought into the world by sin, the mediation for which our Lord offered Himself! "I am poor," He says, "and in labours from my youth. I am ready for scourges and my sorrow is continually before me. I can die but once, but I will offer Myself on ten thousand altars, appearing daily before My Father as Priest and Victim to make intercession for My brethren. They may assist at My Sacrifice and appropriate My merits. I will live amongst them as one of themselves, and daily, if they desire it, will come into their hearts that by uniting My joys and sorrows with theirs, these may have value for eternal life."

His atonement need not have been at this cost. A prayer, a tear, would have sufficed for our Redemption, had He so willed. Yet has He done more than was necessary to gain our love?

To the generality of men, even those who call themselves Christians, it seems nothing so very wonderful that God should lay down His life for us; that under the appearance of bread He should live in our midst to the end of time and give Himself to us as our food. We come into the world and find this provision made for us nineteen centuries ago. We accept the result, so far as it appeals to us, and there, for the greater number, the matter ends.

What it must have been to suffer as He suffered during His whole life with the knowledge that so many would make Him no return! "Jesus needed not that any man should tell Him, for He knew what was in man." He knew there was not one ache of pain of body, not one pang of His soul too much—there was no waste, nay, there was not enough of pain and the love to which pain testifies, to pay the price we set upon our hearts.

We must be a problem to the Angels. The almost incredible love of God for men which fills them with astonishment and rapture, we take as if it were a matter of course. We know that from eternity God has loved us and decreed that we should be sharers in the divine Nature, as St. Peter says, and co-heirs with Christ. That when we had frustrated the designs of God and forfeited our stupendous privileges, His love led Him to pity rather than to punish. He could not bear to leave unbridged the gulf that separated us from Him, and sent His Son to reconcile us to Him and re-communicate to us the divine life. We know that as Head of the Church, His Mystical Body, He does not consider Himself complete without us, nor will till at the consummation of the world all the members of the perfected body will be in full communion with the Head. Meanwhile His very life He pours continually into it.

And yet the sense of loneliness is wont to oppress many of us on our way to God, the belief that we tread alone a narrow ridge, sheer down from which fall precipices on either side. No one can stand with us; a little in front, perhaps, or a little behind, but beside us as guarantee and surety—none. To its nearest and dearest, nay, to its very self, the soul is a mystery, its impulses, its inconsistencies, its ever-varying moods—there is no diagnosing of these.... It is a stranger to itself. What we call self-knowledge leads but a little way through the obscurity and the tangle. How, then, should any other know us as we really are? At times we are conscious of terrific possibilities of evil in ourselves, and perhaps of capabilities of good we fear to contemplate. Thus we journey on, lonely to the end, an enigma to all, to ourselves most of all.

Not so. For One comes forward and offers Himself as a Companion: "And, behold, Jesus Himself drawing near, went with them."[1] Could we have imagined graciousness such as this? From Him we came. To Him we are returning. But that He should also be our Fellow-Traveller by the way! "Behold, I am with you all days even to the consummation

---
1 Luke 24:15

of the world!"[1] With you in Prayer; "Always living to make intercession for you."[2] And with you in daily life as Companion and Example.

Union with Him in Prayer.—We do, indeed, need Him here. And how absolutely does He supply that need! Think of His daily Sacrifice, His daily Visit to us in Holy Communion, if we will; His Presence with us on our altars day and night. In the *Sacrifice* God comes first and I second.—His Glory is the first and chief end. In the *Sacrament* the order is reversed—the primary end is my good, God's Glory the second. My first thought, then, at Mass must be what is due to God—*Adoration, Praise, Thanksgiving, Reparation*—Petition must wait.

And now comes the joyous thought that He Himself is ready to supply all my need. What as yet do I know of *Adoration?* Next to nothing. I call the heavenly host to my help: "Let all the angels of God adore Him." But this is not enough. He alone knows what the Divine Majesty deserves. He must do all Himself. "By Him, with Him, in Him," here is all I need. I may kneel quietly beside Him and watch His Adoration going up like incense from the altar. Straight up it mounts into the heaven of heavens and circles in fragrant clouds around the great white Throne. One is seated there from whose Face heaven and earth flee away; but my adoration—for mine is in that cloud indistinguishable from His—remains, undispersed, undisturbed, nay, accepted and welcomed as adequate.

---

[1] Matt. 28:20
[2] Heb. 7:25

And so with *Praise* and *Thanksgiving*, I watch the fragrant incense mount. My praise and thanksgiving are there. Mingled with His in this moment, the words of the *Gloria* take on a new meaning: "We"—He and I— "praise Thee, we bless Thee, we glorify Thee, we give Thee thanks for Thy great glory." "Thanks be to God for His Unspeakable Gift!"

Reparation. Again I watch that ascending cloud. Therein is all my hope, all my prayer. For it is now His prayer who is our Advocate with the Father, "Always living to make intercession for us." Our cry for mercy and forgiveness go up together. His cannot be rejected, therefore mine is safe: "Forgive us our trespasses." "May this incense ascend to Thee, O Lord, and may Thy mercy descend upon us."

Petition. "I will ask the Father for you," He says to me now. "Ask and you shall receive; seek and you shall find; knock and it shall be opened to you. Now is the acceptable time. You have not because you ask not." But let us remember His own injunction to seek first the kingdom of God and His justice. Let us not restrict our petitions at this acceptable time to the things that pass with time, however needful these may be. We have His promise that if we seek first the good things that are eternal, such as the soul needs for its safety and welfare, "all other things," so far as they are good for us, shall be added unto us. Our Lord bids us ask, but He also reminds us that it is possible to "ask amiss." And He, our Model in prayer who could never ask amiss, prayed in His extremity of need: "Father, if it be possible, remove this chalice from Me. Nevertheless, not as I will, but as Thou wilt."

Such prayer is always safe and is more powerful with God than unconditional petition. And when, especially after Communion, the prayer of our hearts goes up to Him with the pleading of the Sacred Heart so close to ours, we may rely on the Father's Heart to hear and help. When we ask for bread He will not reach us a stone.

Let my prayer, then, ascend as incense in Thy sight, swaying, now and again, as a cold draught affects it, but quickly mounting once more, all its fragrance, all its acceptance with Thee, my God, due to its close union with Him, our Advocate with Thee, the Son of Thy love. To answer for another is not to ignore or slur over what is faulty, but to make common cause with the defaulter. Do this for me, O good Jesus, merciful Mediator. Stand in my stead; undertake my defence; meet all charges against me. Excuse where Thou canst, and where Thou canst not excuse—*forgive*.

When our incapacity and helplessness weigh heavily upon us after Communion, He says to us: "Instead of bemoaning your poverty, see how rich I am making you. My Heart now is yours. Take from It all you need to pay your debt of thanksgiving. Or, if you will, stay quietly by whilst I do for you all that should be done. I know all that God deserves, all that you need, all that you desire for those you love. Leave it to Me; I will see to it. And the quarter of an hour of our meeting over, you will go home enriched in the sight of Angels and Saints, with strength to bear up against temptation, discouragement, weariness, home troubles, the monotony of daily work. My Peace I leave with you; My Strength I give you, not always felt—but there. Lean upon it; trust it; it shall not fail you. Go back to your daily life, not sad in the thought of how little you have done, but with humble thankfulness, relying on what I have done for you. You are not alone; we are going to work together. Turn to Me as the day goes on; ask Me and I will help you in every need. I will think for you, speak by your lips, work with your brain and your hands, pray with your heart."

Union in Daily Life and Work.—"*Per Ipsum et cum Ipso et in Ipso*"—by Him, with Him, in Him, *like* Him, is the orientation the Church gives us every morning, the direction she would give to aim and endeavour. When we work in company with a friend, how often there is momentary interruption by a question or a look. Such union with our Lord as the hours go by is protection, light and strength. Five minutes spent in His companionship—aye, two minutes, if heart to heart—will change the whole day, will make every thought and feeling different; will enable you to do things for His sake that you would not have done for your own sake or for any one's sake but His.

To form the habit of asking: "What would Jesus do in my place; What advice would He give me here?" is to follow Christ not in word and in tongue, but in deed and in truth. Whatever its obscurity, a life so lived is bound to be a great influence for good: "He that abideth in Me and I in him, the same beareth much fruit." This is what He asks of us, that our life be in such dependence on His that He determines our views, stirs our energies, takes into

His hands the leading-strings of our conduct. "It is not the work of one day, nor children's sport," says à Kempis, and it would be unfair to conceal the time, patience, and self-conquest in front of one who sets out on this road, before he can say with St. Paul: "I live, now not I but Christ liveth in me."

It is the road taken by all the saints; the same is open to me. *For me* was that divine yet human life lived. In my poor way I can imitate it—*if I will*. All who truly love Him and own Him as Lord and Master feel they cannot pass by heedlessly what was said and done and suffered for them. *And can I?*

Lord, let me not live my life uninfluenced, or but feebly influenced by that Life of Thine which was lived on earth for me. To be admitted to the Life which is to last for ever in the joy of Thy Presence, I must be like Thee in mind and heart. It is to form this likeness that Thou comest to me in Holy Communion. I must not leave it for the fierce fires of Purgatory to accomplish. It is not their purpose. But the gentle action of Thy Presence with me, during life, O Sun of my soul, will gradually perfect it even here. So has it been with Thy saints; so is it going on daily in Thy faithful servants all around me. So, dear Lord, let it be *with me!*

XII

Trust in His Reward—Himself

"*I will be thy reward exceeding great.*"—Gen. 15:1

"*Father, I will that where I am they also whom Thou hast given Me may be with Me, that they may see My glory.*"—St. John, 17:24

S T. JOHN gives us a sample only of the "many signs Jesus did in the sight of His disciples" during the forty days of the Risen Life. But enough to show His followers of all time that they will find their Divine Master always, as His first disciples found Him after the Resurrection—"only Jesus." Our last glimpse of Him through the open heavens is in the Apocalypse. No other "revelations" to His servants are of faith and we are under no obligation of believing them.

But the "Showings" of Divine Love to our English anchoress, Mother Juliana of Norwich (1373), appeal to us specially for their conformity with the Gospel records of our Lord's dealings with His own during His Risen Life. There is the same wonderful condescension and tenderness in His converse, and in His assurance to His favoured servant that His communications were not for herself alone, but for all her "even-Christians, for their endless comfort and solace." What charmed her most, she tells us, was the union of so much majesty with such sweet homeliness.

"Our good Lord showed that it is fully great pleasure to Him that a simple soul come to Him plainly and homely. It is the most worship that a solemn king may do a poor servant if he will be homely with him. And of all sight that I saw, this was most comfort to me that our good Lord that is so reverent and dreadful is so homely and so courteous. To show to me that am so little this marvellous homeliness is more joy and liking to me than if He gave me great gifts and were Himself strange in manner. It is the most joy that may be that he that is highest and mightiest, noblest and worthiest, is lowest and meekest, homeliest and courtesiest.... The most fullest of joy that we shall have as to my sight is in this marvellouse courtesie and homeliness of our Father that is our Maker and in our Lord Jesu Christ that is our Brother and our Saviour."

Lowliness so clings to Him that it underlies the glory of the Risen Life. According to these "Showings," it appears even in Heaven and renders Him to us, His human brethren, divinely attractive.

We might have thought that weary Heart would have been glad to leave the earth and men, to feel as He bowed His head in death: "It is finished!" Yet how did He return to us from the grave? With more than the exultation of friend or lover: "I am risen and am still with thee, Alleluia."[1] At the Ascension, as if loath to quit the world He so loved, He

---
1   Easter Sunday, Introit

must needs leave His footprints on Olivet. "He hangeth about us for tender love," says Mother Juliana. "There is no creature that may wit how much and how sweetly and how tenderlie our Maker loveth us.... He standeth all alone and abideth us continually, moaning and mourning till when we come. And He hath haste to have us to Him for we are His joy and His delight. And thus shall He be as long as any soul is in earth that shall come to heaven; and so far forth that if there were none such soul in earth but one, He should be with that all alone till He had brought it up to His bliss. . . . For we are not yet one with our Lord. And though some of us feel it seldom, it passeth never fro' Christ till what time He have brought us out of all our woe...."

"Then said our good Lord asking: 'Art thou well apaid [content, satisfied] that I suffered for thee?'

"I said, 'Yea, good Lord, gramercy, blessed mote Thou be.'

"Then said He: *'If thou art apaid, I am apaid. It is a joy, a bliss, an endless liking to Me that ever I suffered passion for thee; and if I might have suffered more I would have suffered more.'*

"He said fully sweetly this word: *'If I might suffer more.'* He said not: 'If it were needful to suffer more,' but *'If I might suffer more.'* For though it were not needful and He might, He would.... All that he doth for us and hath done and ever shall, was never charge to Him.... *'If thou art well apaid, I am well apaid.'* As if He had said: *'It is joy and liking enough to Me, and I ask not else of thee of My travel, but that I might apay thee.'*

"And in this my understanding was lift up into heaven where I saw our Lord God as a lord in His own house to which He hath called all His own dear worthy friends to a solemn feast to solace them with joy and mirth full homely and full curtlessly in endless love.

"God showed the bliss that each soul shall have in heaven that willingfully hath served God in any degree on earth.... Our Lord said: 'I thank thee of thy service and of thy travel.' The thanks that he shall receive of our Lord God is so high and worshipful that methought all the pain and travel that might be suffered of all living men might not have deserved the worshipful thank that one man shall have that wilfully have served God. He maketh his service known to all that be in Heaven and all the blessed shall see the thanking...and him thinketh that it filleth him though there were no more."

How is it that the "Four Last Things to be ever remembered" are so seldom called to mind? And that the last, which concerns us most, is for the greater number, even of Christians, practically lost sight of altogether? Death and Judgment are the work of an instant. Yet because for believers their result is momentous and everlasting, they do occasionally recur to mind, and, perchance, have some influence on conduct. Hell, in the ages of Faith, had a distinctly deterrent influence at the critical times which call for its warning. But that which is to last for ever, the Home waiting for us as soon as we leave this place of preparation—how often do we give it a thought? The first Christians had their conversation continually in Heaven.

So had the anchoress of Norwich, and with the King of Heaven, to whom she spoke as friend with friend.

"I saw," she says, "three manner of longings in God. The first is that He longeth to learn us to know Him and love Him ever more and more. The second is that He longeth to have us up into bliss. The third is to fulfill us of bliss and that shall be on the Last Day. Then shall we see verily the cause of all the deeds that God hath done. For some of us believe that God is all mighty and may do all; and that He is all wisdom and can do all; but that He is all love and will do all—there we fail.... Desire we, then, to trust in Him mightily for the more that we trust, and the mightier that we trust, the more we worship and please our Lord that we trust in."

Trust is the beginning and the end of all her "Showings." She used to speak to our Lord in prayer with the greatest simplicity, telling Him of any difficulty she had about the life to come. "Our good Lord answered to all the questions and doubts that I might make, saying full comfortably:

" 'All shall be well, and all manner of thing shall be well.' Ah, good Lord, how might all be well for the great harm that is to come by sin to Thy creatures? I had no other answer of our good Lord but this: *'That which is impossible to thee is not impossible to Me. I shall save My word in all thing, and I shall make all thing well.... Thou shalt see thyself that all manner of thing shall be well.... I may and I can and I will make all thing well and thou shalt see thyself that all manner of thing shall be well.'"

Although the joy of Heaven will be beyond anything the eye can see, or the ear hear, or the mind conceive, it will not overpower our poor little soul but be exactly what He who made it and knows it through and through sees will satisfy its every need, bring it a happiness prepared specially for itself and fill its cup of joy to the brim. "Not only," says Mother Juliana, "He taketh heed to noble things and to great, but also to little, to low, and to simple. And so meaneth He in that He saith: '*All manner of thing shall be well,*' for He will that we wit [understand] that the least thing shall not be forgotten."

Not a single desire of our heart but shall be satisfied by the love of our Heavenly Father in the Kingdom *prepared for us* from the foundation of the world. "Our reason," she says, "is now so blind and so low, that we cannot know the high marvellous wisdom, the might and the goodness of the blissidful Trinity. And this meaneth He when He saith: 'Thou shalt see thyself that all manner of thing shall be well.' As if He said: 'Let Me alone, my dear worthy child; intend to Me. I am enough to thee. Take now faithfully and trustfully, and at the last end thou shalt be verily in fulhead of joy.' It longeth [belongeth] to the royal lordship of God to have His secret counsels in peace, and it longeth to His servants for obedience and reverence not to will to know His counsels. When we be all brought up above then shall we clearly see in God the privities which now be hid to us. And then shall none of us be stirred to say: 'Lord, if it had been thus it had been well.' But we shall all say with one voyce: 'Lord, blessed mote Thou be, for it is thus and it is well. And now we see verily that all thing is done as it was Thine ordinance before anything was made. In Thy love Thou hath done all Thy works and in this love thou hast made all thing profitable to us.' In our making we had beginning; but the love wherein He made us was in Him from without beginning. And all this shall we see in God without end."

Joy will pour into the soul by every avenue; will be compensation for every sacrifice; satisfaction for all its affections, for memory, understanding and will, and after the resurrection for all its spiritualized senses. The words so often repeated in Scripture that God is faithful, it will find fully realized. "Know ye that no one hath hoped in the Lord and hath been confounded.... Believe God and trust in Him, and your reward shall not be made void."[1] "There hath not failed so much as one word of all the good things that He promised."[2] Nothing has been accounted too insignificant for recompense; the fidelity of our God has stored up all against "the Day of reward." And that Day is the Day of Eternity which knows no evening, no lowering of the intensity of its calm transports of joy. When, then, our insensibility here and now weighs heavily upon us, let us look forward to the never-ending, never-wearying thanksgiving that is to come. The hour is drawing near when *all that is within me* will bless God with such intensity of fervour, such enthusiasm of praise, such delight and pride in Him and in His glorious Perfections, that it will need the strength of an immortal spirit to sustain the vehemence of its ardour. As the ocean must relieve its fullness by the

---

1 Eccles. 2:4, 6, 8
2 3 Kings 8:56

rising of its waters into the heavens over every inch of its surface, so will my heart need the everlasting "Sanctus," the merging of itself in the vast harmony of creation's praise, to enable it to bear the torrents of joy and love and thanksgiving which the face to face Presence will bring to us when our God shall be all in all!

There may have been seasons in our lives which seemed to satisfy our thirst for happiness, but they passed quickly and left behind an aching void. And there are spiritual joys which God sends from time to time to give us a taste of the freedom and happiness to come. But not for us to rest in, for we have not here a lasting city but look for one that is to come—*Expecto!*

Final Perserverance

God has His good and His best and His perfect gifts. His best gift to us is Final Perseverance, because it crowns all the rest. Without it these will not only avail us nothing, but will turn to our greater loss. No one, says the Council of Trent, can with absolute certitude be assured of it, but God never refuses it to those who ask it, and we must have the firmest trust in His help to complete in us the work He has begun, provided we ourselves are not unfaithful to His grace.

The means to obtain from God this precious grace which will put us in secure possession of all He has in store for us, of the Inheritance and Reward, which is Himself, are *prayer* and *daily perseverance*—that is, daily fidelity. The greatest of graces which cannot be merited, He grants—not to any kind of prayer, but to that which is persistent and earnest. "Hold fast that which thou hast," says our Lord; "he that shall persevere to the end shall be saved." We hold fast by frequent recourse to the Sacraments, the healing and the life-giving—Penance and the Eucharist. "They shall draw waters with joy from the Saviour's fountains." "He that eateth this Bread shall live for ever." "In the Eucharist," says the Church, "a pledge of future glory is given to us." At the Elevation in the Mass the priest holds up to the Eternal Father the whole stream of the Precious Blood. There are those who take that moment for asking the grace of Final Perseverance. Can we think it will fail them?

Daily perseverance is the road to Final Perseverance: "Be thou faithful unto death and I will give Thee the crown of life." We complain that we are merely plodding on—stumbling, falling, rising, tripping, again and again. "The just man shall fall seven times,"[1] which he could hardly do unless he rose quickly. "Come to Me, child, and I will put you right again." Oh, if this were not the character of our Heavenly Father—what would become of us! He will bring to a good end the work of our life if that work has been done for Him, that is, with a view to please Him; and if we are found plodding on when our call comes, all will be well with us.

Perseverance, says St. Thomas Aquinas, requires a greater firmness of soul than valour. "The patient man is greater than the valiant." Who does not know this? When duty is obscure or monotonous how prone we are to get wearied and cast down.

---

[1] Prov. 24:16

"What is patience?" a priest asked a class of children.

"Please, Father, to hauld on," said a little child.

It is not the beginning, but the ending, that marks a work. The holy Curé of Ars used to say: "All is well if we carry our cross well"; for this is to bear it bravely and implies a serious following of Christ.

Not even a saint's life could be fairly shown in diagram by a steady upward line. Like the "jumpy chart" of a feverish patient, it is a succession of ups and downs. Let us "carry on," then, in patience and in trust; every effort, every Sacrament and prayer brings us nearer to God.

"*Let them trust in Thee who know Thee,*"[1] says the Church.

"I know in whom I have believed," says the great Apostle, "and I am certain that He is able to keep what I have committed to Him."[2]

My God, give me the trust in Thee which Thy promises call for; which Thy goodness to us deserves; which My experience of Thee justifies.

How God, our Father, Redeemer, Sanctifier, does plead with us for Trust! Through all the revelations of Himself—the Father—in His messages through the prophets and His patient training of His people for the Redeemer they were to give to the world; the Incarnate Word, who with His own lips would speak to us and teach us, and live and suffer with us as one of ourselves; the Spirit of Love, whose working in the early Church is so vividly set before us in the "Acts

---

1 Gradual of Septuagesima Sunday
2 2 Tim. 1:12

of the Apostles" that they have been aptly described as the "Acts of the Holy Spirit"; the continual action of Father, Son and Spirit through the history of the Church, the Lives of His Saints and the workings of His grace in the secret experience of every one of us—how from the beginning in Genesis to the consummation of the Apocalypse it is one long bidding for our trust!

All His Perfections—Omnipotence, Wisdom, Justice, Love, His Tests and His Inspirations, His Perpetual Presence and assistance are at our service to invite the confidence of our poor hearts.

And how loath we are to give it—taking back incessantly what we have but just surrendered. Is not the restless ocean a figure of our inconstant hearts? On every coast the world over it is flinging its waters only to reclaim them on the returning tide, except where here and there a daring wave has ventured too far to be recovered. Oh, that our trust could once for all so fling itself upon the inviting Shore as to lose itself there for ever!

When our eyes open in Eternity to the dealings of God with us through life, how we shall cast ourselves upon Him and bewail our miserable mistrust, and marvel at the Patience that has borne with us! "Too late," shall we cry with Augustine, "too late have I known and loved and trusted Thee, my God! Yet not too late, for I have Eternity wherein to repay Thee, and give Thee at last, at last, what from Eternity Thou hast sought—the trust of Thy child!"

Additional titles available from
St. Augustine Academy Press
Books for the Traditional Catholic

Titles by Mother Mary Loyola:
Blessed are they that Mourn
Confession and Communion
Coram Sanctissimo (Before the Most Holy)
First Communion
First Confession
Forgive us our Trespasses
Hail! Full of Grace
Heavenwards
Holy Mass/How to Help the Sick and Dying
Home for Good
Jesus of Nazareth: The Story of His Life Written for Children
Questions on First Communion
The Child of God: What comes of our Baptism
The Children's Charter
The Little Children's Prayer Book
The Soldier of Christ: Talks before Confirmation
Trust
Welcome! Holy Communion Before and After

Titles by Father Lasance:
The Catholic Girl's Guide
The Young Man's Guide

Tales of the Saints:
A Child's Book of Saints by William Canton
A Child's Book of Warriors by William Canton
Illustrated Life of the Blessed Virgin by Rev. B. Rohner, O.S.B.
Legends & Stories of Italy by Amy Steedman
Mary, Help of Christians by Rev. Bonaventure Hammer
Page, Esquire and Knight by Marion Florence Lansing
The Book of Saints and Heroes by Lenora Lang
Saint Patrick: Apostle of Ireland
The Story of St. Elizabeth of Hungary by William Canton

Check our Website for more:
www.staugustineacademypress.com

www.ingramcontent.com/pod-product-compliance
Lightning Source LLC
Chambersburg PA
CBHW020002050426
42450CB00005B/285